SUPER
CONFIDENCE
ACADEMY

SUPER
CONFIDENCE
ACADEMY

A How To Guide For Parents, Teachers, Mentors, Martial Arts Instructors And Coaches, To Understanding And Building Confidence In Children And Anyone Who Needs It.

By

ARTHUR HEARNS

Copyright © 2018

LEGAL AND COPYRIGHT

Copyright ©2018

DEDICATION

This book is dedicated to the following people:

To my parents, Deborah F. Hearns and Arthur Porter, for always believing in me and continually building and reinforcing my confidence, throughout my life. Thank you for planting the seed of "anything is possible if you put your mind to it and believe in yourself."

To my sons, Arthur and Nathan, you were made exactly how you were supposed to be made, so never let anyone tell you that you are not good enough, because you are. And, with confidence, perseverance, and desire, you will not only become the person you want to be, you'll also achieve any goals you set your heart and mind to.

An abundance of confidence lies within every person, to attain it, all you need to do is give yourself per-mission and set it free.

~Arthur Hearns

FOREWORD

What separates those who succeed from those who fail? This is a question I ask myself quite often. I am an African American doctor, double board certified in Internal medicine and Nephrology (a doctor who specializes in the care and treatment of kidney disease) who also has a Masters in Public Health specialized in Health Education and Behavioral Science.

I have had quite a journey on my way to becoming a physician, and have faced numerous barriers and challenges to get to where I am today. Truthfully speaking, if I had to pinpoint one trait that has been necessary and vital throughout my life to become truly successful, I would have to say it is the ability to maintain my own self confidence.

When I was in medical school there were numerous times that were tough. Concentrating had always been an issue in my life. I am pretty sure that there were many people who thought I was an undiagnosed case of ADHD (Attention Deficit Hyperactivity Disorder). Despite that, I believed in myself, fought and worked hard and found numerous ways around it.

When I was doing one of my first clinical medical rotations ever, I was so excited and I studied hard to excel to get ahead. Despite all my work and effort, I had one faculty instructor, a pretty important one, tell me that they did not think that I was cut out for medicine, and that I should probably choose something else in life. Initially, I was pretty disappointed.

But more so I was actually shocked, that this person who was supposed to serve as a guide to inspire and motivate me to do better, essentially just tore me down and tried to break my spirit. She attempted to dictate and tell me what my own limitations were.

What she didn't realize was that I had a boat load full of self-confidence, and nobody was going to tell me what my limitations were. She didn't realize that throughout my life I had a number of positive role models, some teachers, some mentors, but my parents espe- cially, who instilled in me the point that I determined my own limitations in life, and in that I had no limitations in life. I determined my own self-worth and no one could put limits on my own poten- tial. They helped build my self confi- dence so that I could not see any barri- er ever stopping me. When I had my mind set on something I was going to accomplish it without fail. Those are principles which I live by to this day, and the reason why I never give up and have never given up on anything.

Self confidence is necessary to allow you to go past your own limits in life to proceed to excellence. The goals you set for yourself can only be accom- plished if you believe that you can achieve them. One needs confidence to carry out any and every challenging task in life. The difference between having it and not having it is crucial to having the outcome that you desire. Athletes need it when they play sports, you need it when you take tests, when you interview for a new job or for entrance to a school, when you audition or perform in a play, or the school band. It is involved and is important in every aspect of your life.

Having confidence impacts the way you are viewed and what decisions you choose to make. Often time the risks people choose to take on in life is a reflection of how confident they feel they will be successful. It can be a measure for your self-esteem. It will directly affect how you present yourself and how you are viewed by others.

So here is the funny thing about confidence that many people do not realize because it is somewhat subconscious, it takes work to maintain it. It is surprisingly all to easy to bring down someone's confidence. You could easily fail a test, lose a race, be made fun of by your peers, and one's self esteem, the confidence you have in yourself can be shattered.

Without confidence you can be constantly filled with self doubt and your own happiness could be challenged greatly. Having positive role models in your life versus negative ones can completely shape someone's self esteem and your abilities to remain confident in difficult situations. Maintaining your confidence takes strength in your character, and by having positive role models that can say the right words at the right time, or demonstrate that they believe in you. That in itself can do wonders for developing your own abilities to stay confident at critical times. Getting young people and adolescents to believe in themselves could inspire greatness beyond measure. This brings me to why this book is important and is a must read, if you aim to inspire others.

I have known the author of this book, Arthur Hearns for the last 17 years. He's one of the most focused, positive and inspirational people that I have ever known. He's genuinely interested and has dedicated his life to helping the people around him. He is an entrepreneur who owns martial arts schools, and provides education in fitness and nutrition.

The work he does every day enables and affords both kids and adults the tools and knowledge to increase their own self-confidence and self worth. He has written this book to help guide both kids and adults who are seeking to become role models to groups of others, and has provided the foundation on how to go about doing so.

Super Confidence Academy is a necessary requirement for any teacher, leader or role model trying to inspire, cultivate and build confidence in children and adults. This book can be used as a tool kit to help leaders and role models develop a solid framework for building the skills needed to do this at a very high level.

If it were not for the positive role models and mentors that came into my life, who helped to instill confidence and the drive to overcome challenge after challenge, I may not have had the chance to become the doctor I am today. I would not have had a chance to provide care to the incredible patients I have seen all these years, or had a chance to attempt to inspire those around me and those who have trained under me.

This book will help you become a leader that motivates and brings about positive change in those around you. You will want to read every page to get the golden nuggets that are being offered that can be used to positively impact someone s life. It is worthy investment of your time and energy, and the skills you gain will undoubtedly be ones that you will keep forever. Enjoy!

~ Kobena Dadzie MD MPH

INTRODUCTION

First, I would like to thank you for your support in purchasing my book.

Truth-be-told, this is not my first attempt at writing a book. In fact, I have many manuscripts that have escaped completion. However, I look forward to bringing those books to life, once I gain confidence from completing my first book.

It was important to me that the words in these pages remain as close to my thoughts and ideas, as possible. Even though, I had this book edited to "smooth out" the flow, I made sure to keep the message, as a genuine as possible, so you know that I am directly speaking to you. Since, I am not a professional writer, forgive me if you happen to find typos or grammatical errors. And, feel free to message me with anything that stands out to you.

Entrepreneur, Allan Nation once said, "The secret to change is first understanding why things are the way they are." I wrote this book with that concept in mind. It is my goal to help you understand "why things are the way they are," so you can make important changes in your life.

My other goal is to help you take a deeper look at your confidence level, so you can better understand the importance it plays in your personal and career success. The objective is to strengthen your confidence and improve the areas that that need a little extra TLC.

I developed the Super Confidence Academy after teaching children and adults, martial arts and fitness. During this time, I observed many things about both younger and older people, as it pertains to confidence and character-building.

This experience, a lifetime of people-watching, and me being the person I am (a person, who enjoys observing people - their personalities and behaviors), my hyperawareness of my own feelings, and my own confidence or lack of, in

various situations, has given me incredible insight, which I share in this book.

The concepts shared in this book may not be unique, but they have been helpful to me and many of my students, young and old, as well as their families. In addition, being married and having two children has provided me with even deeper insight into how confidence is developed and maintained. And, how the seeds we plant in our children, from the beginning, influence their confidence levels, and who they will eventually become, as adults.

The *Super Confidence Academy* is a guide on how to overcome the fears that keep a child from being his most confident self. I cannot stress enough that the key to a successful and healthy life is confidence. Therefore, the aim for this guide is to help you strengthen, build, and rebuild your confidence.

This book will teach your child how to correctly identify various types of confidence, so he has the tools needed to live his life with fewer regrets, more friends, and everything he wants in life. Honestly, I believe that confidence is a type of mental muscle that gets stronger when you put it through the confidence-building perseverance cycle (CBP). *What is the CBP cycle?* Well, it involves *trying*, *failing*, *finding* the courage to try again, and *repeating* that cycle until you succeed and gain the confidence you are lacking.

I believe that failure helps a child's confidence muscle grow. All she has to do is get through the trauma, move past the failure, and try again. I know, easier said than done. But, guess what? It's 100% doable. For example, if your child tries something new for the first time like riding a bike, and can go a good distance without falling on the first try, she is going to feel more confident about riding her bike in the future. As a result, she will celebrate this victory.

You can also celebrate this victory, as her parent. In other words, you can praise yourself for your child's accomplishments, and still know that she is not yet proficient at riding a bike. She still needs more practice, so you wait until she becomes more proficient at riding the bike, before you take her for an ice cream reward. You know from experience that your child will most likely fall a few times before she is "good" at riding her bike. And, guess what? Falling is a good thing! In other words, falling is a necessary part of learning how to ride a bicycle. Moreover, it is both natural and inevitable.

It is the "I did it!" feeling that builds confidence, so to build real confidence, one must fall. To be clear, it's not the "fall" that gives your child confidence, no, it is strength, perseverance, a will to succeed, and courage that gets her back on the bike afterwards. Therein, the real victory lies in getting up again – after failure. *Okay... so, what keeps people from building strong confidence muscles?* **FEAR!**

The antithesis of confidence and perseverance is **fear**. But, the act of trying and failing builds the immunity needed to overcome this **fear**. Don't get me wrong, it's okay to be afraid, from time-to-time, but the key is to not allow it to overtake you (i.e. run your life). If you've ever heard the term "frozen with fear," it usually refers to a short period; however, this isn't temporary for some people.

No, for some, the **fear** is frozen for a longer, more significant time. Fear can keep you *stuck*. More specifically, it can prevent

you from going outside of your comfort zone and trying something new. When a person becomes "frozen with fear," it prevents him from trying again, and, as a result, he is unable grow, improve, or succeed.

Therefore, for your child to become great at building and rebuilding his confidence, and venturing beyond his natural ability (i.e. physical skill), he needs a coach or trainer – someone, who can guide him through the tough parts, mistakes, and failures. More specifically, he needs someone, who can give him a much-needed pep talk and prepare him for life, so he doesn't learn that it is okay to quit, thus, leading to weak "confidence muscles." This book is for the "trainers" (i.e. parents, teachers, martial instructors, coaches and/or those, who work with children on a regular basis.

Make sure to go to our website:
www.SuperConfidenceAcademy.com

Also ask to join the closed FB group at:
https://www.facebook.com/groups/
SuperConfidenceAcademy/

To download the SCA Worksheets mentioned throughout the book.

PREFACE

This book was created to help people develop more confidence. After years of working with families, children and adults, in the fitness and martial arts space, I noticed that so many people lacked confidence in themselves. The strange thing was that some individuals were confident in one environment or at a particular skill but not in others. Over the years I realized confidence could be broken into categories of different types.

This got me to start reflecting on my own life, past experiences and those around me to gain a deeper understanding of this special power called confidence.

It seemed that confidence, above all of the other major life skills and character traits, was the one that you could grow up to become an adult and never develop it to a level you are happy with. Unlike other these other traits, confidence cannot be faked. It is very difficult to hide that fact that you are not confident. Someone can pretend to be kind, focused, disciplined or have self-control.

I also noticed a connection between happiness and confidence and success and confidence. Most of the very successful people I know, have an abundance of confidence. They also have many friends and live life with little regret of missing out. Truly happy people also have a confidence about them that radiates out to others. Being confident allows us to take advantage of and create more opportunities in life.

By sharing my knowledge and understanding of this topic in book form, I am hopeful that it will help many more people. This book is for parents, teachers, coaches, instructors, life coaches, managers, trainers and any person who wants to develop and inspire confidence in themselves and others. With this book we can help people start developing well rounded confidence when they are young so that they can become successful, happy adults that have healthy, experience rich lives.

I want to thank and acknowledge all of my students and their families, my family, my children, friends and everyone who has helped me learn more about confidence.

TABLE OF CONTENTS

Dedication   IV.

Foreword   V.

Introduction   VIII.

Preface   XI.

.

1. Who Needs the Super Confident Academy?

2. Confidence...The Foundation of Character

3. Will Having More Confidence Make a Difference?

4. Nine Categories of Confidence

5. A Personal Lesson in Failure

6. It Takes a Village to Raise a Child

7. Why is My Child So Shy?

8. How Can I Build More Confidence in My Child?

9. Can Teachers Have a Significant Impact on a Child's Confidence?

10. From Super Shy to Super Confident...Is It Possible? Is It Necessary?

11. What Can Take a Person's Confidence Away?

12. The Fear of Making Mistakes and Trying New Things

13. Learning to Speak Up for One's Self

14. How Can I Prevent My Child from Becoming a Blind, Quiet Follower?

15. The Confidence to Stand Up to Bullies

16. How Does the Martial Arts Build Confidence?

17. Do All Martial Arts Build Confidence?

18. Sports and Coaches

19. You Were Born with the Confidence and Perseverance of a True Champion!

CHAPTER ONE

Who Needs the Super Confidence Academy?

"Confidence is a powerful, courage-like, inner strength and belief in yourself that gives you the understanding that you will succeed with time, preparation, and perseverance. It allows you to overcome your fears, both known and unknown, try new things, and express your thoughts and feelings."

~Arthur Hearns

Confidence is one of the most malleable and volatile powers humans possess. Both children and adults have this ever-fluctuating energy. Confidence is neither fixed nor set in stone for life. You can gain it and lose it, throughout your childhood, adulthood, and later years.

And, during your formative years, you're much more sensitive to relationship "influencers" like parents, teachers, coaches, and friends as well as environmental "influences" such as parties, school,

work, and the way you interact within your community. All of these things can affect your confidence.

Confidence is also important for character-building. But, just like other traits, it needs to be developed. The only difference is that other traits change frequently - usually progressing, maintaining, and/or changing throughout your life, as you mature and gain life experiences.

And, even though, confidence plays a significant role in your life, as a parent, mentor, teacher, and/or coach, it plays an even bigger role in your child's life. Of course, respect, manners, self-control, and courtesy also play important roles in your child's life, most of which he learns at home from his parents and extended family.

It is common, as you age, to realize just how crucial it is for you to practice manners and respect every day, in public – even if you don't practice those same traits behind closed doors. The good news is that most people behave appropriately and demonstrate enough respect for others to carry them throughout each day. On the other hand, think about how many people don't say "Good Morning" or "Hello" to you, even when you say it first. *Are they rude or just lacking confidence?*

It is important to understand that even though you can't overlook confidence, you also can't allow it to remain underdeveloped. *Why not?* Well, a lack of confidence prevents you from being the best "you," you can be in life (i.e.

Making friends, getting great jobs, and/or feeling successful at your job). A strong confidence, on the other hand, prevents you from experienced regret about things you may have missed out on.

If you are confident, you don't have to watch others do what you wanted to do, but were too afraid to try, because you didn't have the confidence to make it happen. Truthfully, confidence is underestimated, especially in comparison to other life skills and character traits. And, while the other traits are highly important, confidence is the trait needed to raise a child, and instill her, the confidence she needs to be successful in this world.

Carefully think about the words you use in front of your child and the language you use when speaking to her. Also, be mindful of our child's confidence, so you uplift it, instead of crushing it with your words. Confidence is sensitive and delicate. It's easy to have a breakdown, and once it occurs it's mighty hard to rebound. You can't just press rewind after you've said something hurtful to someone else, because once those words are out there, they can't be taken back.

In addition, there may have been times when you said something soul-crushing to someone, and as a result, the other person experienced a dip in confidence. *And, guess what?* You may not have even known you hurt the other person's feelings. The smallest things can have a huge impact on others. More specifically, you have the power to either zap someone's confidence or strengthen it. The good news, however, is that a dip in confidence doesn't have to be permanent.

On the other hand, if you decide to wallow in your failures and mistakes, you will remain stagnant - unwilling to expose yourself or even try, because of something that happened to you in your past. So, even if you think the words you said mean nothing, the truth is your words have the power to change lives. That is why confidence "sculptors and protectors" must think about the things they say and know what not to say.

It is also important to note that there may be extreme cases, where a person experiences other horrible events like: sexual molestation or domestic violence or other forms of physical and mental abuse. These terrible situations affect your confidence, mental stability, and emotional state. In these cases, people are usually advised to seek professional counseling for the trauma. And, many times, psychiatrists prescribe psychotropic drugs (i.e. antidepressants and anti-anxiety meds) to help ease the emotional pain of witnessing or experiencing trauma first-hand. The truth is some people never really heal from the damage.

Then, there are the health challenges that some people face. You may not know this, but health challenges like autism, attention deficit disorder (ADD), attention deficit hyperactivity disorder (ADHD), dyslexia, and speech impediments can also affect a person's confidence level. I mention this because not all journeys to building confidence are the same. Yes, they all start at the base of the "Fear Mountain," but it is the individual, who determines if this mountain is simply a speed bump or a barely reachable, massive mountain like Mt. Everest. Fear also lies in your mind – what you think you can do and who you think you are.

And, although, some obstacles are harder to overcome than others, the key to conquering these road-blocks is to believe in yourself and keep going – and going – and going. Still, the process is the same every time, and it will work the same every time – when the time is right for you and you are ready and willing to adopt this new state of mind. Once you have the "right" mindset, you can climb the "Fear Mountain" without fear.

So, to answer the question at the beginning of this chapter, the goal of this book is to help you understand the true meaning of confidence, so you can better understand it's importance in your life. Therefore, the *Super Confidence Academy* aims to teach you how to increase your confidence, so you are prepared for any situation that arises. This is a reference manual, guide book, and how-to-book all rolled up into one. Ultimately, this book will teach you how to repair and rebuild your confidence, when it has fallen or dipped below normal levels, due to the stresses of life.

It was created for parents, teachers, coaches, martial arts instructors, and anyone, who works with children, or knows of someone, who needs help building his confidence. It is designed to help children learn how to climb the "Fear Mountain," overcome it, and reach new levels of confidence.

Make sure to go to our website:
www.SuperConfidenceAcademy.com

Also ask to join the closed FB group at:
https://www.facebook.com/groups/
SuperConfidenceAcademy/

To download the SCA Worksheets mentioned throughout the book.

CHAPTER TWO

Is Confidence the Foundation of Character?

"With realization of one's own potential and self-confidence in one's ability, one can build a better world."

~Dalai Lama

I bet you can think of many character traits and life skills that you possess, am I right? Did you know that confidence is one of the foundations for personal development? Well, it is! In fact, when it comes to pre-

senting and practicing good character traits, confidence is the foundation and respect is the main pillar.

In other words, think of confidence, as the driving force or battery that powers the other character traits, so without confidence, you can't fully embrace and practice the other character traits. Keep in mind, however, that the aim is to not only develop a healthy confidence for your child, but also foster it in others. So, it's important not to be too confident aka cocky. When a person is truly confident, he understands that every journey may not be successful. He also understands that failure is intertwined with self-improvement. So, ultimately, confidence centers on being "okay" with your mistakes, and working towards fixing them with certainty.

The difference between confidence and arrogance/cockiness is that the arrogant/cocky people don't believe they can fail or make mistakes, so when it happens their egos are bruises, and they become immobilized with fear. My goal, however, is to help develop and shape well-rounded individuals, who have superb characters. *Why?* Well, because when you have more confidence, it's much easier to accomplish your goals.

Listed below are ways that character traits are related to, and need the support of confidence:

Courtesy & Respect

If you aren't confident, you may not feel comfortable looking others in their eyes. In addition, you may not know how to use your words to effectively communicate with others, and there's a good chance, you'll refrain from speaking freely in front of groups, because you lack the **Confidence of Voice**. It is common for others to perceive someone, who lacks confidence, as being "awkward," "distant," or even "cold," when, in actuality, he isn't *trying* to be disrespectful. He is "shy," so he isn't able to socially interact with others at a level that society deems "appropriate."

Perseverance

If you aren't confident, you'll continue to go full-steam ahead, even when you know it's a mistake. You'll most likely adopt an "I can't...," or "quitters" mentality. The truth is a person's confidence needs to be strong enough to overcome his failures and mistakes.

Physical Strength

If you don't physically feel strong and healthy, you will *not* be able to obtain a high level of confidence. In other words, if you don't feel as skilled or talented, as others, you'll lack the confidence needed to be successful. More specifically, a lack of confidence can influence how you see yourself and your physical abilities.

Goals-Setting

Confidence influences your goals. *How?* Well, when you don't have confidence, you are more prone to setting "easy" and "simple" goals. In other words, you won't take risks for fear that you won't be successful. Therefore, you'll most likely "play it safe" and stick to goals that you can achieve them.

Purpose

Without confidence, it's hard to figure out your purpose in life. But, when you discover your purpose, your confidence level soars.

Mindset

Believe it or not, your mindset affects your confidence. Factors like: emotional control, overcoming adversities, doubt, fear, thought processes, worry, are all connected to your confidence. So, if you are dealing with "things," your confidence may be negatively impacted.

Relationships

Relationships are important. In fact, developing healthy relationships/ friendships, forgiving those, who have hurt or disappointed you, communicating with a variety of people, and practicing good manners are ways to strengthen your confidence. If you don't have good relationships with people, your confidence will suffer.

As you can see, many character traits are connected to confidence. A low level of confidence prevents other characters traits from reaching their potentials. The best way to wrap your head around the function of confidence is to think of it, as a "supercharger" that gives you a much-needed boost, so you can complete your tasks and accomplish your goals.

That is why it's so important to help children develop a variety of confidence "types." Because, honestly, there are many different "types" of confidence. And, it's these different "types" of confidence that help you become a respectable human being with an outstanding character.

Guess what? You can have a stellar work ethic and be a good communicator, but if you lack confidence, you're not going to accomplish, as much as you could have accomplished, if you had had a strong self-confidence. In other words, if

you're not confident now, you probably weren't confident, as a child.

CHAPTER THREE

Will Having More Confidence
Make a Difference?

"Noble and great, Courageous and determined, Faithful and fearless. That is who you are and who you have always been. And understanding it can change your life, because this knowledge carries a confidence that cannot be duplicated any other way."

~Sheri L. Dew

Absolutely! Children are constantly developing, growing, and learning. So, if you plan properly, you can plant the seed of positivity, and then cultivate the positive traits that you'd like your child to possess. **Note:** It will take time for the attributes to fully develop and "bloom." It requires patience, perseverance, and persistence.

Figuratively, children are equivalent to sprouting plants that need to be watered, fed, and immersed in sunlight. It's important to nurture these "seeds," just like I referred to in my video, *The Gardener*. In addition, when these "seeds" are exposed to too many negative experiences aka weeds; it hurts their growth and developed. Because, just like plants, humans are *moved* by negative vibrations and emotions. More specifically, these vibrations can inhibit the physical growth of plants, thus, preventing mental and emotional growth in people, and leaving them void of confidence.

On the other hand, positive vibrations and environments can promote healthy development and growth. So, create a happy, healthy, and safe environment for your child. So, encourage confidence-building by providing a "safe space" for your child.

The ultimate plan for child-rearing is to create, plant, and nurture healthy attributes that can grow and develop in your child. It is important to prepare her for a more successful life journey. Children are mentally pliable during their formative years, so it's easier to shape and mold them, so they develop healthy mindsets, when they are young.

So, I have organized the nine different types of confidence, and in **Chapter 4: Confidence Types**, you'll learn how people are influenced by these "types." You will also learn how to improve and strengthen these confidence types.

Confidence is a very, very powerful force. It's an amazing inner strength that helps you achieve more and get more out of life. It also touches your relationships, academic success, social life, career, finances, etc. In fact, it's very possible that your child may be confident in one or two areas, but not in others. Therefore, the best way to deal with your child's lack of confidence is to help her improve in those areas.

When your child has natural confidence, she does better at school, at home, and with friends. When a shy child goes somewhere for the first time, she probably gets nervous or becomes afraid to interact with others, which is completely natural. More specifically, it's an instinctive protection mechanism for survival. If the child doesn't know the new people, she becomes fearful of them. More specifically, her brain does what it needs to do to protect her from possible harm.

In addition, a child, who lacks confidence, may try to hide his face, so others don't recognize him. He may also divert his eyes away from the "possible" predator. On the flip side, a confident child may be brave, because he knows that his parents will protect him from danger. This is a type of confidence that occurs when you know your parents have your back. Therefore, a confident child will look at others, make eye contact with them, have fun, and smile. He will also look at the faces of others, and talk to others – even if he doesn't know them all that well.

On the other hand, a child, who lacks confidence, won't even lift her heads, or may start crying, if someone makes eye contact with her. It's important to note that it's common for young children to avoid eye contact and exhibit

shyness, especially in new environments, and in new settings with new
adults. But, thankfully, this can be easily
conquered.

Ultimately, having confidence can
help your child in a variety of ways.
More specifically, a confident child will
most likely be exposed to more opportunities. Because, let's be honest, confidence makes most things a little easier.
When you have confidence, you are willing to try more, do more, and go more
places. And as a result, you are most
likely to go further in life, then if you did
not have confidence.

The tricky part about confidence,
however, is that it's sensitive and fragile.
It's also flexible, moldable, and shape-
able. Therefore, it needs to be handled
like nitro-glycerin. In addition, confidence can be built up, and instanta-
neously broken down - just like that! So,
it's important that you work on building
and maintaining your child's confidence.
Just remember, a confident child will
grow – mentally, physically, and even
spiritually.

Moreover, the more you demonstrate confidence, the more your child will exhibit that same trait. Maintaining this type of positive attitude and mindset expands your child's potential. In other words, she is more inclined to reach high levels of success and popularity, if she has confidence. It's possible, however, that a person with low self-confidence, who read a lot, kept to himself/herself, and learned how to write programming codes, as a child, is now a successful computer programmer or software developer. But, even that child, who grew up to be a highly successful adult, probably had some level of confidence in himself and his abilities.

Truth-be-told, there's nothing wrong with being shy and not having a lot of confidence. Your child can still grow up and make a good living, BUT to get the most out of life - the fullest experience, it's imperative that he have confidence. Therefore, your goal should not only be to help your child reach a healthy level of confidence and maintain it, but also to prevent this newfound confidence from becoming arrogant or cocky.

This is where the "The village" part comes in. Your role is to keep your child on the "right" path, teach her humility, and prevent her ego from inflating. You see, sometimes, a child exhibits behaviors that you, as the parent, must correct or critique. There may also be times when you have to break your child's ego down, so she can be "rebuilt" and become a productive individual.

Now, I'm not suggesting you "break down" your child in a degrading or abusive way. But, in life there will be times when you must let your child know there is a better or healthier way of thinking and behaving. In other words, you may need to explain to your child, her mistake, and demonstrate a better way to handle the situation.

But, be prepared – she will most likely suffer from hurt feelings. Because, even when the best athletes or the smartest individuals make mistakes and teachers correct them, it stings a little. But, after a while, your child will appreciate the corrections, because they will ultimately improve her skills, leading to a stronger self-confidence.

Still, failure and mistakes hurt. So, teach your child how to pick himself up and keep going. Try again. Teach your child to be like the people, who view failures and mistakes like small, pesky mosquito bites – knowing that something happened, but not allowing it to interfere with their days, instead of others, who unfortunately allow the sting of failure to hit them with the power of a Mack truck.

A healthy confidence will help your child bounce back, move past the failure, and get back on track, so he can achieve his goals. Because, the sooner, he can do that, the faster he'll bounce back, the further he'll go, and the more self-worth he'll have.

The truth is, when you have a high self-confidence, you are in a healthier mental and emotional state. You also don't waste time wallowing in self-pity or self-doubt for too long. AND, you have a more positive outlook on life. Furthermore, you accept failure and rejection without blaming others for it.

People with a healthy level of confidence also have more friends, than their counterparts. *Why is that?* Well, people with confidence are exposed to and take advantage of more opportunities. They also tend to take more chances and have fewer regrets. Therefore, with confidence you live a more fulfilling life.

CHAPTER FOUR

Nine Categories of Confidence

"One important key to success is self-confidence. An important key to self-confidence is preparation."

~Arthur Ashe

I have categorized confidence into nine different categories. This idea came from observing people (children and adults) over years and noticing how they displayed various levels of confidence in different situations. More specifically, I have observed people, who were completely confident in one type of environment or life situation, but had zero confidence in a different type of environment or situation. These were not situations that required a specific skill or special training. For instance, it would make sense to need a specific skill or special training to play a sport, however, when it is something like speaking in groups, dancing at a party, or mingling with new people, it can be challenging for some people.

Nine Types of Confidence:

1. Confidence to Overcome Fears (COF)

Applying courage to the things - i.e. fear of the dark, trying new foods, etc. that scare you

2. Confidence to Face Your Failures (CFF)

Having the perseverance to try and try again and again

3. Social Confidence (SC)

Being confident in groups and around people

4. Confidence of Voice (COV)

Using your words and voice freely

5. Physical Confidence (PC)

Demonstrating confidence through your body language – i.e. gestures and skills

6. Confidence of Self-Image (CSI)

Being comfortable in and with your body

7. Creative Confidence (CC)

Believing that your thoughts and ideas count and anyone can create

8. Confidence of Will (COW)

Believing you can do whatever you set your heart and mind to

9. Confidence of Intelligence (COI)

Identifying what you feel proficient in. What is your passion?

These nine categories can be divided into three groups: physical, mental, and both. It is important to note that there will be situational overlaps for some of these categories. For example, **COF** and **CFF** can apply to the same situations. There may also be a situation that could apply to more than one of these categories. Lastly, there could be situations that are isolated and unique to any of the categories listed above.

There is another type of confidence, which I label as **False Confidence.** I do not include this in the list above because it is the one we want to avoid developing. It is not one we want to spend time or energy on trying to build or improve. We will talk more about False Confidence later in the book.

So, let's go over the categories, so you understand how to

recognize and identify the confi-
dences that need building or repair-
ing:

Category 1:

Confidence to Overcome Fears

This type of confidence is something you begin developing during your earliest years. As an infant, there were probably things you were afraid of, or uncomfortable with.

Confidence of Overcoming Fears is another type of confidence. The type of fears mentioned here differ from the fears mentioned earlier. If someone lacks creative confidence, he may be afraid to create. **Confidence of Overcoming Fear** refers to things like being afraid of the dark, a fear of heights; a fear of riding a bike for the first time, etc. Overcoming fears is BIG, primarily because children are naturally more afraid of things, than adults. In fact, some children, who were afraid of things like dogs, swimming, or the dark, are still afraid of those things, as adults, because they never learned how to face and overcome them.

For more information, download: *"Confidence Building Cycle of Perseverance"*at www.SuperConfidenceAcademy.com or on the private FB Group with this link, https://www.facebook.com/groups/SuperConfidenceAcademy/

The only way a parent can tell if her baby is afraid or uncomfortable in a social setting, is if the baby cries. But, once the baby grows and becomes a toddler and then adolescent, she learns how to express her fears in more diverse ways. But, by this time, if she lacks, **Social Confidence**, she starts hiding behind her parents' legs or bodies. This child hides her face from a new person, people, and/or a group of people. She also refrains from speaking, because she is shy.

With more **Social Confidence**, however, she makes friends easier she's not afraid to interact or play with other children. When children have **Social Confidence**, they learn how to build the skills needed to make friends, form relationships, and connect with others. And, along the way, they also learn to either face their fears or overcome them. The truth is parents have a way of reassuring children that it is safe to face things that scare them, because they are usually harmless. But, learning to face and overcome fears can be a difficult task, depending on the fear. For example, your child's fear of riding a bike for the first time is different than his fear of the dark or of large dogs. The good news is there is a formula to overcoming fears. And, *all* fears require the same process, regardless of the fear.

The difference lies in the time it takes for someone to work through the process. It is important to understand that that time is completely up to the individual. This reminds me of a quote by Dan Sullivan, in which he says, *"There are two types of suffering, long-term and short-term, which one you experience is up to you."* What this means is that when you can get to a point, where you are ready to face your fears, it's time to follow a fear-busting formula. Keep in mind that there's usually an underlying cause of low confidence.

The following formula is designed to build your child's confidence by eliminating the fear that is currently occupying the mental space designated for his confidence. Therefore, I have included a detailed explanation of the concept of **Overcoming Fear Formula (O.F.F.)** at the end of this chapter. The **O.F.F.** formula is important for improving your child's confidence level, because it involves a series of steps that can block or eliminate fears.

Understanding Your Fears

Understanding the various types of fear can help you better understand how to overcome them. But, *what is fear? Well, the textbook definition of fear is:*

FEAR: noun -

1. An unpleasant emotion caused by the belief that someone or something is dangerous, likely to cause pain, or a threat.

2. A feeling of anxiety, concerning the outcome of something or the safety and well-being of a someone.

3. The likelihood of something unwelcome happening.

There are four major types of fear outlined here: Misplaced Fear, Floating Fear, Real Fear (reaction to real danger), and Social Fear.

Floating Fear is a fear that has no foundation. It is unrealistic, but floats in your mind, because you're afraid of something. Still, there's no real cause for it. In other words, past experiences do not warrant this type of fear. It's something you have imagined. For example, you tell a colleague, "I don't want to go on stage in front of this crowd, because I'm afraid I'll mess up and they will laugh at me." Well, if that's never happened before, then there's no reason for you to think that, so you're creating the worst possible scenario in your mind, which is making you afraid.

A more positive spin would be to say, "Hey, I'm going to go in front of this crowd, and blow them away with my skills!" Well, that may have never happened before either, but at least it's taking you in a positive direction. It's putting you in a *growth mindset*. Any time you face your fears, and/or do something new, your brain says, "Let's grow!" In other words, when you step out of your comfort zone, you're priming yourself for growth and success.

So, think differently about your fears. Instead of being afraid of a negative possibility, visualize the opposite. The visualized, positive scenario has never happened to you before either. It is better to focus your energies on the outcome you would prefer to have happen than on the one fear. *Teach your child to ask herself which outcome she'd rather have happen?* Then, remind her to stop letting the fear "freeze" her. Then, encourage her to step outside of her comfort zone, so she can learn what areas need "fixing," and which ones she excels at. Explain to her that stepping outside of her comfort zone will help her feel better prepared for whatever life throws at her. Then, tell her that with practice, she will accomplish her goals.

Misplaced Fear is a type of **Real Fear,** but this fear tends to appear at all the wrong times, keeping the person "frozen," and preventing him from trying new things. For example, let's say your child is deathly afraid of the dark. Being afraid of the dark is a real, natural fear that some people have. Interestingly, it's an evolutionary protective mechanism that has kept humans alive for centuries.

A child, who is at home with his family, and is afraid of the dark, knows that there are no strangers in her house, yet, he remains afraid of the dark – even with a protective dog like a pit-bull sleeping beside him. So, if you ask your child to go upstairs to put on his pajamas – alone at night, he will most likely say, "No, I'm too scared." This is especially true if he is 3 or 4-years-old. However, by the time he turns 7- or 8-years-old, he will be old enough to understand that he has a **Misplaced Fear** of the dark.

Remember, to a young child the fear is real. So, try harder to change your child's mindset about his fears. For example, explain it like this, "I understand that you're afraid of the dark and I **know** your fear is real, but the best way to conquer it is to think about it in a different way and face it head-on. In other words, think about your fear (of the dark, for example) by reminding yourself that we are right around the corner. We can hear you – we can *always* hear you, and if you need us, we'll be there before you can blink twice. There's no reason for you to be afraid of the dark in your own house."

"This is where your family lives. This is where your dog lives. If there was something or someone in the house, the dog would hear it, smell it, and then attack it. The dark is scary to you, because a long time ago people didn't have houses and lived outside in huts, tee-pees and tree houses. These people *had* to be afraid of the dark, because there were predators, animals, and dangerous people roaming that could be a threat to their safety."

"Plus, there weren't any laws or even locks on the doors to protect them from harm. Therefore, their brains learned that they couldn't see in the dark, so they needed to be afraid. As a result, a fear of the dark was born. That mentality has been passed down from generation to generation, but you don't have to worry about that now, because your home is safe."

Social Fear, is a fear, centered in doing things, in groups or around people. If you have a **Social Fear**, you are afraid of socializing and making friends. You also lack **Social Confidence**. **Social Fear** is closely related to the **Floating Fear**. If you'd like to interact with others, but you are too afraid to do so, then you most likely are experiencing a **Social Fear**.

So, for your child to overcome her fears, she must identify the root cause of the fear and address it head-on. The key is to do those things is confidence. Teach your child that to conquer her **Floating Fear,** she must reframe her thought processes. In other words, instead of thinking of everything that could go *wrong*, she should focus on what could go *right*. And, to conquer her **Social Fear**, she needs to determine what is causing the fear and remind herself that there is nothing to fear – they are just people – people, who make mistakes and have faults just like her. They just want to learn more about her, because they find her interesting, but if she doesn't feel comfortable with them, then she can always move on and make new friends.

Category 2

Confidence to Face Your Failures

The word "action" translates to having *persistence* and *perseverance*. In other words, it's having the spirit to try again and never giving up on goals or tasks just because you are not successful the first time. When you give up, you stop moving forward, and if you stop, you never reach your goal. In other words, the only *real* failure is giving up and quitting.

Teach her how to bounce back from mistakes - quickly. When you allow your child to sit in those negative emotions, instead of prompting her to get back up and try again, you're giving her time to build a case for quitting. According to "village elders," while your child is in such a state, valuable time is wasted, and she can't get better or improve. In other words, progress can't be made with such a mindset.

More specifically, she can't improve when she is in a negative emotional state. This is especially true, when she is in a self-deprecating state. She'll only become frustrated, angry, and defeated. For example, your child may become aggressive, while learning to tie her shows, if she has a hard time tying the laces. She may pull out the laces or throw her shoes, because she is frustrated. Your child acts out because she can't figure how to tie her shoes.

When your child allows frustration to dominate her mind, she is prevented from successfully complete her task. This mindset continues and filters over into other areas of her life until she resets her mind and releases the negative energy. This is true for both children and adults. *So, if your child tries to work on something, but can't and then becomes frustrated, guess what happens next?* Well, the more frustrated she gets, the more she's not going to be able to finish her project or perform to the best of her ability.

Therefore, it's important to teach your child how to use that negative energy and emotions, as fuel to motivation her. In other words, instruct her to take that energy and convert it into useful and positive energy. You can do this simply by explaining the following the diagram to her with the goal of having your child eventually do these steps by herself.

Listed below are six steps to overcoming failures and mistakes:

Step 1: Acknowledge It

Have your child acknowledge his mistake or failure. Then, have him say, "I'm not getting this right now, but I will!" Then, take a break and work through the remaining steps.

Step 2: Accept It

Explain to your child that it is okay that he is having a challenging time. Help him understand that this is an opportunity to grow and improve, but the key is to keep his mind clear and free of negative emotions.

Step 3: Understand Why?

Why is your child having a hard time? Maybe, because the challenge or task at hand is new to him. This new skill, like anything new, can be challenging. Remember, even the best tennis players in the world face challenges, when they switch to a different activity like ping-pong or basketball.

Step 4: Prepare for Success

Have your child visualize that he is completing the task-at-hand and/or developing a skill needed for success.

Step 5: Make a Plan

Have your child make a plan for what is needed to make his vision a reality. Get him a coach, teacher, or assistant, and watch videos or listen to audiotapes that will help your child better grasp the topic, material, or skill.

Step 6: Just Do It!

Now, it's time for your child to get back to work with a new outlook and a clear mind.

Category 3

Social Confidence

Social Confidence is having confidence in groups and around people. The truth is many adults and children are deficient in this type of confidence. If you have a healthy level of **Social Confidence**, you aren't afraid to go into a room full of people or join a party or meeting. You also feel comfortable interacting with a variety of people. In other words, you can mingle without anxiety or stress.

Are you terrified to speak in front of people?

Are you afraid to talk to new people?

Do you feel awkward at gatherings, because you don't know how to socially interact in group settings?

It is common for children to avoid activities because they are super-shy. If your child is one of those people, and he's afraid to interact with his peers. He most likely has a **Floating Fear**. Remember, this fear has no real foundation. It is more of a mental and psychological hiccup than a *real* threat to a person's well-being. In extreme cases, however, this fear can last for a very long time. It can also interfere with a person's ability to make friends and build relationships. *And, guess what?* If you lack **Social Confidence**, you're probably also filled with **Social Fear**.

The good news is that your child can build up his **Social-Confidence**, but first, he has to eliminate his **Social Fear**. All he has to do is follow the six steps in the **O.F.F.** (**Overcoming Fear Formula**). For more information download our char on SuperConfidenceAcademy.com.

You may not know this, but there is a spectrum when it comes to the stages of development. I have been a martial arts instructor for over 16 years, so I have witnessed every possible level of confidence. I have also helped individuals, from every part of the spectrum, improve their confidences. I've seen children cling to their parent's legs, crying and scared to participate at birthday parties or group events. As a result, the parents often became embarrassed and frustrated, and left. I've also seen children, who were fearless. These children walked into the parties or events like they were "bosses." They ran around, breaking all of my rules, and tearing stuff up! They had no regrets, and they didn't care about anything or anyone. They were not shy in any way.

Most children, however, fall on a natural and healthy part of the spectrum. Some are timid, overly cautious, and "hard to warm" towards others, and others are outgoing, social butterflies. These children jump in line first, raise their hands first in class, and walk up to others and introduce themselves first. Then, there's the big middle area on the spectrum, which is also good. These children exhibit **Social Confidence**.

What if your child arrives at the playground and there are already children playing there? Will she have the confidence to walk up to the other children and start playing with them? Will she have the confidence to ask one of the other children, if she can join in and play? And, will she have the confidence to introduce herself to other children?

Social Confidence is also closely related to and can overlap with **Physical Confidence** and **Confidence of Self-Image**. For example, your child attends a birthday party, and the other children start dancing. Maybe she has no problem interacting and dancing with the other children. But, then suddenly, your child, who has an above average **Social Confidence**, begins to show reservation. She suddenly becomes resistant to the idea of dancing in front of people.

So, what happened? Well, she probably experienced a decline in her **Confidence of Ability**. More specifically, she probably became worried that the others would make fun of her or she will look silly, if she danced in front of her peers. So, even though, she is normally confident, in general, maybe she was unsure of her dancing ability, and therefore, unwilling to take the risk. It is important to note that if she did decide to dance and then became embarrassed, because her peers laughed at her, it could potentially affect her current level of **Social Confidence**. And, causing her to decline future party invitations. This is a perfect example of a strong **Social Confidence** with a low **Confidence of Ability** or belief in oneself.

I have witnessed this discrepancy many times. It usually occurs during the birthday parties held at my martial arts school. Certain children will walk into the party, talk to everyone, and be have the best time. These children don't show any signs of shyness or a lack of confidence. But, then, we'll announce the next game, the "Freeze Dance," and suddenly, these formerly confidant children stand completely still – not moving at all! They won't dance or do anything. They just stand there staring at you. So, I'll ask them, "What's going on? Let me see your moves."

And, they shake their heads like, "Umm…no way, I'm not dancing!"

So, there's a fear there, and... Where there's a fear, there is a lack of confidence. The children know this fear is not a fear of danger or bodily harm, but they're still afraid that something's going to happen to them, if they dance. Perhaps, the children are afraid that the other children are going to laugh at them or make fun of them. Regardless of the exact cause, this fear involves a lack of confidence in a physical skill - dancing.

There are also cases when a child is confident in one physical ability and not another. For example, a child excels at the "Freeze Dance," but then it's time to try a new drill or game like "Jump Laser Rope," where she must run under the rope at the "right" time without getting hit by it and she becomes deathly afraid to do it, because she doesn't want to "mess up." More specifically, she doesn't want to be the one, who doesn't make it. So, as you can see, there are many types of confidence. When you can understand the differences and how they affect your child in each situation, you can help him strengthen his confidence in these areas.

Category 4

Confidence of Voice

Having a **Confidence of Voice** is when you use your voice to speak freely - without holding back. Your voice can be a powerful tool...if you use it correctly. That is why it's crucial that your child develop a **Confidence of Voice**, as early as possible. This type of confidence will allow him to express himself through his words. On the extreme end, it provides him with the power to stand up for himself against bullies. On the other end, it provides him with the ability to ask for the things he needs or wants.

It is important to understand that some people, and especially children, will not ask to go to the bathroom or for a glass of water, because they are afraid to speak up. When I was in elementary school, one of my classmates was extremely shy – so shy that he wet his pants, because he was too afraid to ask to go to the bathroom. *Well, guess what?* This happens quite a bit with children, ages 5-to-7. And, in some cases, it happens even later than that.

These children lack the confidence to ask for what they need or want. *How can you stand up for yourself against abuse, ask for a promotion, give a presentation, or ask someone out on a date, if you're afraid to speak up?* You can have strong **P.C.**, **C.O.F**, **C.C.**, and still go your whole life without a **Confidence of Voice**.

Truthfully, this may be the most important type of confidence, when it comes to safety and self-defense. The other day, one of the moms from my academy listened to me give a lesson on **Confidence of Voice** and shared how valuable my lessons are to her child. This mom felt that more children and especially young girls need to hear lessons like this. She said, "If more little girls heard these lessons, maybe there wouldn't be a need for a *#Metoo* movement."

I understood exactly what she meant and thought what she said was powerful. I hold *Women's Self-Defense Seminars* and the two most important things I emphasize are: awareness and using one's voice with confidence. It is important that children feel confident enough to say, "**NO!**" They need to have the confidence to stand up to bullies, or so-called friends, who are pushy or just mean. Children need to be confident enough to speak up for what is right and just, regardless of the situation.

So, encourage your child to use her voice, when she feels uncomfortable. And, encourage her to ask for the things she needs. But, most of all let her know that it is okay to express her feelings, especially to her friends and family. Using her voice in this way will give her what she fears she will lose – **RESPECT**.

When you tell people how you feel, they will, at least respect you for having the courage and confidence to do so. So, even if they make fun of you, they know how difficult it was for you to use your voice and because of that, they will respect you for it. And, every time you use your voice, in an effective way, you gain new confidence points. You also start to feel more confident about the power behind your words and voice.

Everyone feels better when they express themselves in a healthy way. The feeling of regret and frustration for holding back words and ideas can have long-lasting negative effects on your psyche. Then, these feelings can turn into emotional baggage that is too heavy to carry. So, devote time to helping your child develop this type of confidence.

*Listed below is an exercise you can do with your child build her **C.O.V.**:*

Have your child write a short letter to at least one person about something she has been holding in and wanting to talk about with that person, but was too afraid to address.

Have her do a few rewrites to get her point across concisely. Then, have a trusted friend of hers proof-read it to make sure the idea is clearly communicated.

Next, have her give the letter to the intended person. Make sure your child explains to that person why she is giving it to her. Then, have your child ask the other person to read it. Your child can say something like, "There's something I have wanted to say to you, but I've been having a hard time finding the right words and courage to bring it up."

4. After the person reads the letter, tell your child to give her an opportunity to think about her words, before continuing the discussion. If the person is up to it and comfortable talking about the topic right then, then that is okay too.

Category 5

Physical Confidence

Physical Confidence is a belief in your physical abilities and potential to learn and improve physical skills. This is closely related to **Social Confidence**. Many people are afraid to try new skills, learn something new, or perform in front of others, because they are afraid of being embarrassed. But, there is only one way to overcome the self-doubt that accompanies a lack of **P.C.**! Nike said it best, *"Just Do It!"* Because, the only way to get better at some-thing and to increase self-confidence is to practice it repeatedly.

The more you do it, the better you'll get. For example, if you perform a task numerous times, your brain and body adapt to it, and you become more proficient at it. But, if you have self-doubt or are too "afraid" to do something, it usually stems from past experiences. It is important to note that you may not remember or know the reason, because it comes from very early in your childhood. It is also important as "The village" to be creative and find ways to try new things. If I tell my students that I believe in them, and that they can achieve any task they put their minds to, it's a good start.

I also let them know that it may take more than one try; in fact, it may take ten or more. I also tell them that they may have to do the job a different way to complete it. That way if they aren't successful on the first try, they don't mentally and emotionally check-out. I want to keep them in a state of courage and determination, for as long as possible. For example, when breaking boards with students at *Hands of Life Martial Arts*, sometimes it takes a few tries to do it. Sometimes the students are afraid to hurt their hands or feet, so they don't put all the pieces together for proper technique – i.e. they don't hit the center of the board, the board holder is not stable, etc. My goal, as their teacher, is to ensure that the students break the boards somehow. It doesn't matter if they stomp on them, jump on them, or kick them - whatever it takes.

I need for my students to have that victory – for themselves! That is why I build them up and place in their minds the confidence to accomplish this task. I let my students know that there is a chance it may not happen that day, but they can always come back tomorrow and try again. I want them to succeed. *Why?* Well, because when they have doubted themselves, this instant change in confidence is priceless. You can see it on their faces and in their body language. This new confidence is downloaded immediately into their minds. And, my goal is to make this happen as often, as I can.

Confidence in your physical ability is trying a new physical activity and having the resilience to handle it, even if you make a mistake, you can't do it, or you're no good at it the first time. This confidence makes you keep going even when it's new to you or you make mistakes. It's also this type of confidence that makes a huge difference in your growth and progress. You've probably heard the story about Michael Jordan not making his high school varsity team. Now, I'm not sure how accurate the story is, but the message and his practice habits are definitely accurate. Apparently, Michael Jordan practiced like 500 or 1000 jump shots a day.

He viewed not making the varsity, as a failure, but found the ability to bounce back and use it, as motivation to get even better. If he wasn't the best, he was one of the greatest to ever play the game. Michael Jordan was a natural, but even that wasn't enough to put him above the other senior players. He needed something more. He was in a competitive environment, where being natural just wasn't good enough. In other words, being a natural is great, but it can only take you so far.

I once read that natural athletic ability only takes you through the first three-to five-years in competitive sports. Then, someone, who is merely average with the proper training, can and will surpass you. As a coach, I want to work with someone, who knows the game better, who's got the drills and skills down-pat, someone, who has been working to be the best he can be, and someone, I can see the development and changes in. Lastly, someone, who shows me that he wants to improve, get better and better, and are hungry to play the game.

Yes, a natural athlete has a gift, but if he is lazy, and doesn't want to make himself better, then he is not going to be a player I want on my team. More specifically, if a natural player is lazy, doesn't want to get better, and I can't motivate him to *want* to do better, then it's going to be hard to shape him into greatness. Therefore, I'd prefer "Grit over Gift."

Category 6

Confidence of Self-Image

Confidence of Self-Image is a very powerful type of confidence. It's the ability to accept your flaws and still be happy with yourself. Self-image is how you view yourself. If you don't view yourself in a confident way, then you'll carry a certain amount of hesitation, regret, and fear. Therefore, it's important that your child develop a positive self-image and make it match her real life. A good way to see if her self-image is accurate is to have her ask her friends and family members to describe her strengths and weaknesses. BUT, only have her ask those, who she really trusts to help her with this exercise. Download at: www.SuperConfidenceAcademy.com.

How to use the **Confidence of Self-Image** worksheet:

Have your child ask 3-to-10 trusted people to help them with the following exercise on **Sheet 2: Confidence & Relationship**.

Have them give each person a sheet to complete it.

Remember, this is your child's trusted person's point-of-view/opinion. It is not fact or definitive of who they are or can be. That is why they should ask more than one person.

Although this exercise is helpful, the answers are *not* important. The truth is that anyone can change in an instant. So, a person's point-of-view/opinion of your child AND their own view of themselves are not fixed or permanent.

This sheet is mainly used to prove that people, in general, have skewed views of themselves. Many also have negative self-images that are usually inaccurate. But, the truth is everyone has some positive traits and strengths. And, guess what? Most of the time we don't give ourselves credit for them. And, here's the biggest issue with self-image - people tend to only focus on the negative things, magnifying them in their minds, and thereby, diminishing their positive character-istics.

But, it's a human's ability to focus on and find the negative aspects, because long ago it helped us sur-vive. Ultimately, we had to identify the negative factors and avoid them to survive. And, that is why people today avoid situations of harm, shame, and embarrassment. We are really avoiding "pain" – pain that is psychological and emotional, but not physical or dangerous. This is a **Misplaced Fear**.

Category 7
Creative Confidence

Creative Confidence is the belief that you can achieve and accomplish new goals and develop ideas from scratch. The other type of confidence is the **Confidence to Create**, which occurs when it's time for you to do something new that you've never done before like starting a business. If you start a business, it may not be a unique business, but it may be unique to you, because you created it. More specifically, you have created the business the way you want it. You decided what the logo was, what you were going to sell, what it was going to look like, and who you were going to hire. But, regardless of all that, you were confident enough to take on this new venture - something that's new to you - something you created from scratch. Truthfully though, this was probably difficult.

Why was it difficult? Because, all you had was a belief in yourself that you could create anything you put your mind to. That is the only way these types of thoughts come into fruition. If you don't have that, then you have doubt. And, when you have doubt, these things take more time to make, or they never get made altogether.

Therefore, helping your child find his confidence to be creative, try new things, draw a picture, create an invention, design a product, create a company, or write a book is important to his development and growth. So, if he's afraid to do these things, then the strategies in this book will help him. This book will teach you how to help your child overcome confidence-zapping fears.

Category 8
Confidence of Will

The categories listed here involve a lack of belief in one's abilities. It's confidence that provides you with the power to believe in yourself, so you don't give up. The **Confidence of Will** is closely related to perseverance. It means not having self-doubt and is synonymous with willpower. Ralph Waldo Emerson's quote is a perfect fit for the **Confidence of Will**. It says, "To be yourself in a world that is constantly trying to make you something else, is the greatest accomplishment."

Confidence of Will and Confidence of Self-Image both fall in the category of believing in yourself and having self-esteem. These mindsets center on maintaining an "I can/I will attitude." They are some of the most important mindsets that one can have. To be successful and reach goals, you must believe in yourself. This confidence involves feeling secure and comfortable with who you are, as a person. It includes everything from how you look, your hair, your clothes, knowing you can achieve the things you, and never allowing self-doubt to get in the driver's seat. But, in my experience, this is the type of confidence fluctuates the most. It comes and goes all the time, in people of all ages. There are only a few rare individuals, who never doubt themselves. They go and go and go and never miss a beat. They are on the extreme end of the spectrum.

Many people, however, experience this fluctuation. It shows up when they want to do things like interview for a job or get a promotion, make more money, try out for a school play, open a business, ask someone out on a date, or just make a new friend. This fluctuation causes them to doubt themselves and think or say things like, "Oh, I don't know, what if I'm not good enough or they don't like me?" *Why wouldn't they? Why are you afraid to talk to that girl? Why are you afraid to introduce yourself to someone and make a new friend? Why are you afraid to go after that promotion? Why? Why doubt yourself?* **Just do it!**

What's going to happen? You get rejected? Maybe. The fear of rejection and being denied or turned down really stings. It feels like a failure. It's a mistake and mistakes sting. But, those wounds strengthen you. So, even though there's pain, it is a pain that makes you stronger. And, the more you do it and deal with it, the better and stronger you get. You also learn what you need to avoid, so you don't experience that type of "pain" again.

This type of confidence can really help your child develop in this area, because there is a chance he made that mistake or failed because he didn't know what to do or how to do it. He wasn't knowledgeable in that area. He had no idea. Then, he came back and tried again. He gathered the information, and trained himself. He improved. And, his brain went, "Ah, I didn't get it at first, but then I did this... and Boom! It came to me and I came back better."

The next type of confidence is **Confidence of Will** and your belief in yourself. Like I mentioned previously, many children, want to please people. They want to please their parents, teachers, coaches, and in some cases, their friends. And, oftentimes, children want to please their parents most of all - to a degree that's almost unrealistic. The tough part about that is there is a difference between parents, and teachers, coaches, and friends. *What is it?* Well, children will often push the boundaries at home. They'll resist more and be more difficult with their parents. BUT, they don't do this as much with teachers, coaches, and friends.

The parent/child relationship is unique in that the child is constantly countering the parent with some type of friction and resistance. For example, you ask your child to clean her room, do her homework, go outside and play, or turn off the electronics and she says, "No, I don't want to." *Am I right?* That's a major part of raising a child. That's just the way it is. Teachers and coaches typically don't get the same type of resistance from children.

These moments of friction add to a parent's gray hair count. You want your child to be healthy and grow up to be a productive member of society. *Why?* Well, because that it's your job, and part of that job entails being patient when tested. More specifically, it means being patient, even when your child pushes boundaries at home and behind closed doors. As a parent, it's up to you to set the boundaries, which is why you need the support of a "virtual village" (i.e. coaches, teachers, martial arts instructors, and anyone else, who plays an important role in your child's life).

Teachers, martial arts instructors, and coaches can communicate with your child in a more direct way with little-to-no resistance. And, as a result, they can get quicker results with a lot less stress, than you, the parent. Therefore, it's important that you embrace this, and communicate with your "virtual village." All you need to say to your "village" is "I need help maintaining the boundaries, rules, and expectations I have for my child, and I would greatly appreciate any support you can provide." When your child realizes that her parents, teachers, instructors, and coaches are aligned, and that she can only function within certain perimeters, she will comply.

Also, when your child becomes aware that the people around her are keeping her in-check, and holding her accountable, she will be much less resistant. You see, by keeping a steady support system in place, you help keep your child in-line and on the "straight-and-narrow." Therefore, by enlisting your "village," you'll have a better chance of keeping your child on the right path and boosting her self-esteem and confidence.

Category 9

Confidence of Intelligence

Confidence of Intelligence involves knowing your strengths and limitations. It's your knowledge and expertise, and what you are capable of learning. This is the mental counterpart to **Physical Confidence**.

Many people shy away from tackling challenging material, because it's new and unfamiliar. Children do it all the time with schoolwork and homework assignments, when they are difficult. Adult also do this. In fact, many adults over the age of 40 find working with the latest cutting-edge technologies and software difficult and/or frustrating. However, both children and adults can overcome these cognitive obstacles. It just requires applying yourself.

Reward your child for overcoming obstacles and reiterate that he did it because he didn't give up. As a result, your child's confidence will skyrocket. This is the best time to start the re-programming phase, so he doesn't adopt this mindset in the future. It is also important to note that adults, who apply themselves, and believe that they can indeed learn to use new technologies, have sharper minds and feel younger than those, who do not feel that they can learn new things. Check out Dr. Stephen Jepsen's, *"Never Leave the Playground"* video.

CHAPTER FIVE

A Personal Lesson in Failure

"All you need in this life is ignorance and confidence, and then success is sure."

~Mark Twain

This story is about my very first bodybuilding show. I knew guys, who were competing, so I decided to try it. I often looked through magazines and was inspired by my favorite bodybuilders at the time. Lee Haney dominated the area, when I was first got into bodybuilding. But, even as young kid, I loved comic books, superheroes, martial arts, and bodybuilding. My father was my first inspiration. He planted the seed for most of the things I really enjoy doing.

When I was younger, I'd watch my dad lift weights, train at martial arts, rock climb, and even tree climb with his friends, and of course, I was right there with them. The more I saw him do these things, the more I wanted to do them. Martial arts and exercising have always been loves of mine. I wasn't a super comic book geek that read every issue that came out, but I did love me some comic books. At the time, I read mostly Batman, Superman, Hulk and Spiderman, but Batman was my favorite - still is!

I also like to do front and back flips off anything I could find. So, I eventually signed up for gymnastics and later, martial arts. I ran, jumped, and climbed every roof, garage, fence, and object in my path...as did many other children back then. We did free-running/parkour before we even knew what it was! And, when I was old enough,

I started working out with weights. I did everything I could to feel, look, and move like a superhero. *Why?* Well, because superheroes are cool, of course!

I started lifting weights in high school, and eventually became one of the best bodybuilders in my division in NJ. But, even with winning numerous state and Mid-Atlantic Championships, I still tried to sculpt my body to look like a superhero. I think this was a driving force for me, as a child. I wanted to be built like Batman or Superman, and guess what? It wasn't even a vanity thing. I liked their positive traits and the good things they did to help people. I admired that and wanted to be like them in my appearance and actions. I wanted to harness their good qualities. You know - be strong and help others.

Well, because I didn't really know what to do and the Internet wasn't readily available back then, I went to the library and looked for information in books and magazines. That's when I learned that I needed to eat more protein, lather my body in fake tanning lotion, and so on and so on. I also needed to go a specialized diet. I was still going to McDonald's, primarily because I didn't know any better. *I didn't have a plan*.

Well, a week before my first show, a friend took me to see this guy named, Derek. At the time, Derek was training at this hardcore bodybuilding gym. And, the first thing Derek said to me was," Have you been dieting?" To which, I responded," Yeah, for two weeks." He then said, "Two weeks?!!" And, I said, "Yes…" to which he said," Well, next time, diet longer." Then, he gave me some specifics.

Derek knew I wasn't ready, but he wasn't going to crush my dreams, so I appreciate that he did that for me. Well, because I wasn't ready and not quite good enough, I didn't do too well the first time. I hadn't been following the proper blueprint for contest prep. I came in 4th out of 5 places.

After that, I watched how the other bodybuilders prepared. I noticed that they had pro-tans (paint-on tans), and oil, which made some of them shredded and super lean. I also noticed how they ate, and how their faces looked drawn and their cheeks sucked in. It was obvious to me that they were doing something I was not. So, I started asking questions like, "How long have you have been eating like that?" Some told me 6 weeks, while others told me a range from 6 weeks to 16 weeks!

It was inspiring and exciting. I continued to ask questions and pick the bodybuilders' brains. I wanted to learn as much as I could to avoid being in poor condition and looking ill-prepared again. I decided that next time; I'd give them my best. I decided that when I went back, it'd be a whole different story. Well, one day, I went to one of the owners of the gym and asked to talk to him for a minute. His name was Mike Duffy, a Mr. America, Mr. New Jersey, and WABBA World finalist. His mentor was the famous bodybuilding coach, Bob Gruskin. So, I approached Mike and said, "Hey, I recently did a bodybuilding show, and learned that I am not ready for them - yet. Can you help me prepare for the next one? I want to get better." He agreed to help me, and then he gave me a workout plan for the off-season. I started training and put on 20-pounds of muscle in 3 months!

This time I had an experienced coach to guide me through the pre-contest prep. He told me exactly what to do - when to eat, when to put on the oil, how much to eat, what percentage of carbs, protein, and fat to consume, and how much cardio to do and at what level. And, let me tell you something – afterwards, I was in the best shape of my life. It was crazy how lean I was. I was so lean that my biceps looked skinless. It grossed me out a little. It was freaky. It looked like I had no skin and my muscles were splitting open! But, thanks to Mike, I knew how to get my body fat off and build quality muscle.

So, then I tried again. I entered another bodybuilding contest. Remember, I went a year earlier (my first bodybuilding contest) and I got 4 out of 5. BUT, this time, I got 1st place! One year after a disappointing showing, I was now ANBC Mr. Teen, New Jersey. What a difference! I could have just said, "Ah, man, I'm no good. I don't know what to do" and just given up. I could have let the poor placement affect me to the point where I didn't try again, or I could have kept trying without coaching – getting me nowhere. BUT, I didn't! I wanted to do it the right way, and with proper preparation and coaching, I became more and more confident each time I competed.

Therefore, believing in yourself is important and being able to bounce back from failures and mistakes is a necessary skill, if you want to be successful. I shared my story as inspiration and motivation for you. If I had never done the first show, I wouldn't have learned how to be better. Also, if I had never done the first show, I probably wouldn't have met Derek, which means there's a chance I never would have learned that I needed to do more to prepare. He primed my mind to be open to learn.

So, teach your child to never give up and always strive to improve at the things he loves to do and the things he needs to do. Encourage him to be as good as he can be. Teach him how to have quick **F.B.B (Failure Bounce Back)** by accepting mistakes and failures, and embracing them, as parts of growing and developing.

CHAPTER SIX

It Takes a Village to Raise a Child

"Confidence doesn't come out of nowhere. It's a result of something, hours and days, and weeks and years of constant work and dedication. "

~*Roger Staubach*

I am not sure of the exact date of this African proverb, but I'm sure it first originated during ancient times. People usually recite proverbs without spending too much time contemplating what they mean - until they are needed. Well, in this chapter, I'm going to focus on what it means to live in a village and experience village life and culture. It is important to note that the further back you go in time, the more you will find close-knit communities or villages. And, most of the time, these villages involved many multi-generation families.

In the past, it was rare for people to leave their villages, unless they were moving to neighboring tribes or villages. So, most families remained in or close to their original village. The fantastic thing about being close to your family is everyone pitches in and helps one another. As a result, all the family members are connect-ed to each other day-in and day-out. Neighbors were either family mem-bers or other neighboring families from the same village. And, every-one worked together to complete tasks. In addition, in the evenings, the families would come together to relax and socialize.

But, what if a baby was born in the village? Who helped her mother with child-rearing and daily duties?

It is important to understand that often, village women helped other mothers and children. The grandmother and possibly the great-grandmother, along with maternal and paternal aunts, cousins, siblings, and friends of the mother, also helped with child-rearing responsibilities and chores. They were excited to spend time with the newest family member. All the women played very important roles in helping women raise healthy, happy, and respectful children.

The village men also played important roles in their children's lives. The men taught the children how to be productive members of society. The children also had many teachers and fantastic support systems that ensured their success. So, these tight-knit support systems not only provided valuable input, but also helped shape the village children, so they'd become upstanding adults. So, ultimate the whole village ensured that the children would be held accountable for things they did. And, they kept the children in-line by disciplining them (just like their own families would) when they misbehaved. This was a very different time than what we have today.

I grew up in Cranford NJ, where I spent a lot of time at my grandmother's house. She lived on Johnson Avenue. At 14, I moved in with my grandmother, so Johnson Avenue holds a special place in my heart. I lived not only with my grandmother, but also my uncles, aunts, great-aunts, great-uncles, and 1st, 2nd, and 3rd cousins. Living with my extended family felt kind of like what I believe living in an ancient village felt like. The other families on my street also consisted of multi-generations. So, if I had to describe it, I'd say it was a modern-day village.

The neighborhood was full of close-knit families and neighbors, who knew each other very well. **Disclaimer:** Just because there were lots of families in the neighborhood, doesn't mean that everyone got along, but they did communicate and respect one another. For example, if you misbehaved and a neighbor saw you, well, they'd most likely tell your grandmother, parents, aunts, and/or uncles.

In addition, non-family members would discipline you, if necessary. In other words, if you were doing something wrong, neighbors would grab you and take you to home, and once there, they'd tell your family what you did wrong, or at minimum, they'd scold you themselves. That's just the way our "village" functioned. And, most times, we learned valuable life lessons and gained invaluable support from our families and neighbors. I remember sitting on the porch with some of the wise, old men in the neighborhood and listening, as they taught me important life lessons. These men also shared their life experiences and wisdom with me.

One of the old men was Jessie Bell or Mr. Bell. Mr. Bell would sit on his porch and talk with both children and adults, while teaching us all about life. Another characteristic of this time was the willingness of neighbors to get involved and help those, who needed guidance and/or help. The cooperative mindset of raising a child in the "it takes a vil-lage" mentality helps children be-come more successful in life, more confident, and just better people, overall. This type of support system teaches children self-awareness and makes them feel connected to the world around them. It also makes children feel cared about and loved. And, as a result, these children de-velop a strong confidence and inner peace. They know there are people, who they can talk to when they to. In a "village" there are people, who are devoted to teaching you, caring for you, and supporting you. The result is a strong sense of security, which is the foundation of confidence.

So, what is confidence? Well, it's being secure in your ability to do things. In other words, it is knowing that you have a support system that will help you, or at least encourage you to keep going. Therefore, security is a part of confidence. The stronger the support team, the more secure/confident you'll be. So, it's important that you, as one of the "village members" support the children in your "village."

I honestly don't mind if a caring neighbor corrects my children, who are misbehaving, and tells them the error of their ways. I also don't mind if my children turn to our neighbors for help, or to learn a skill or life lesson. If a neighbor, coach, teacher, instructor, or even friend can encourage my children, and give them much-needed pep talks in my absence, that's okay with me. Especially, if the neighbor's words of wisdom uplift my children's spirits and build their confidences.

I believe that if we adopt this way of thinking, as a neighborhood, community or town, and as teachers, parents, coaches, and martial arts instructors, it will benefit the children in our communities. It will also provide support for the parents, who need help – even if they won't admit it. Truth-be-told, parents love it when I say to their children, "Hey, make sure you're respectful to your Mom and Dad" or I remind them to say, "Thank you," or I check them when they are being rude to their siblings.

Parents also appreciate the pep talks I give their children, when they're having a hard time in school or someone's picking on them. Ultimately, parents appreciate the support, and the role I play in shaping their children's confidence.

If parents, coaches, martial arts instructors, and teachers get on the same page and work towards the same goal, it will build our children's confidence. More specifically, it will help develop children, who are confident and well-prepared for life. So, it takes a "village to raise a child," which means that we all must be held accountable for shaping the children in our communities - not just when they do something wrong, but when they need help, encouragement, and confidence-boosting.

It's also important that we're okay with other positive people in our community, circles, and "villages" giving a helping hand to us and our children, because raising children is not for the weak of heart and it's nearly impossible alone. Everyone plays a role in child-rearing, whether we know it or not.

Therefore, my goal, with this book, is to bring awareness to the "village mentality" so you can play build your child's confidences.

It's hard to "parent" on your own. And, it's impossible to teach your child *everything*, because the relationship between parent and child is fraught with conflict, friction, and resistance. Truthfully, it's common for children to resist a parent's advice and guidance, in fact, it happens to parents all the time. There are times when your children will listen to you, but many times, when you try to teach your children life lessons, they push back.

The kicker is when someone else says the exact same thing or tries to teach the same lesson and your children act like what the other person said was gospel.

When someone else imparts wisdom, your children listen – no questions asked, but when you do the same thing – it's World War 3. Therefore, it helps to have other "teachers" give those life lessons to your children, especially if they're the exact same lessons you have already given them. These lessons are important, because they reinforce the lessons you, as a parent, have taught and continue to teach your children. So, as a "village," let's help each other. Let's build super-confident children, students, and players, and let's get them ready for real life. The goal should be to help these children become more successful than they would be, if we "raised" them alone - without the support of our "villages."

CHAPTER SEVEN

Why is My Child So Shy?

"Being shy or practicing cautious fear, as a child, is a natural survival mechanism. The problem occurs when a person doesn't outgrow these traits, as an adult. Plant the seeds of many types of confidence, as early as possible, in your child, so she does not miss out on the great opportunities that living with confidence offers!"

~Arthur Hearns

Let's look at the nature of a child. A child is, for the most part, a vulnerable creature, who relies on her parents and caretakers to take care of her. Children cannot take care of, feed, or protect themselves. However, from research in evolution, we know that if something is bigger than us, there's a chance it's dangerous, right? Well, for the most part, children, who don't interact with adults, make eye contact (even up to ages 8 or 9 and maybe into their teen years) probably don't do those things because instinctually their minds tell them that others are bigger, stronger, and potentially dangerous.

And, even though these people may not be dangerous at all, the children's natural instincts tell them to hide and be careful. Honestly, it's usually not a conscious choice. But, with reinforcement and guidance, you can teach your child how to make eye contact, when communicating with adults and peers. Because, there are children, who aren't shy and who display confidence, when it comes to communicating and making eye contact. These children exhibit a type of confidence that comes from a certain level of security and feeling safe. Moreover, they usually feel confident in their families, which make them feel safe enough to engage with the outside world.

Truth-be-told, this type of confidence is rare today with the influx of electronic devices and tablets. In fact, most children spend majority of their time making "i" contact, as in iPads and iPhones, instead of making one-on-one healthy "eye" contact. The truth is "true connections" involves developing genuine relationships, which by-the-way is getting harder and harder to do. Young people are losing this skill at a very fast rate, which, in turn, diminishes many types of confidence. In addition, healthy social communication amongst young people is deteriorating every day. You can even see it in teenagers, who are uncomfortable speaking to adults.

Children can also be shy when interacting with other children. This is because there's a fear of the unknown. When a child is new to a group of children and he doesn't know any of their names, there's a natural fear of the unknown.

In this case, the child is not afraid that someone is going to hurt him or take him; rather he is afraid to get to know the other children. But, if an individual is overly shy to a point where it is interfering with making new friends and developing new relationships, and it becomes an ongoing issue, it can be frustrating. In other words, when it takes too much time for a child to engage and interact with peers or he doesn't communicate his needs or feelings, then it shows a lack of confidence, specifically **Social-Confidence**.

It is up to you and your "village" to help your children develop the skills to move past their shyness.

The good news is that I have included exercises and worksheets that can help you child combat, overcome, and work through his shyness. But, be mindful though, that overcoming shyness is not an instantaneous, overnight process. It takes time. Thankfully, however, I have been able to get shy children past their shyness, so they could break boards. I'd trigger their courage, so they could confidently hit the boards, get excited, and start smiling.

And, although some would still run back to their parents, hiding their faces behind their legs, others would break out of their shells permanently. Those, who would hide their faces and avoid eye contact, were experiencing extreme cases of **Social Fear**. It is important to point out that some children are so shy that they get upset or stressed, when their teachers or coaches highlight or praise them for their accomplishments.

If your child needs confidence-building, you need to figure out what type of praise she will accept. If she experiences anxiety or stress, it could set her back AND increase her fear of being the center of attention. As a result, it could ultimately lower her confidence level. In other words, even if you think you're helping your child's confidence by publicly praising her for things done well, you may be triggering or worsening you're her greatest fear – a fear of attention.

So, as you can see, positive reinforcement and praise can backfire. Therefore, it's important to know if your child can handle public praise. This type of praise makes a child the center of attention, which is terrifying to a child, who lacks **Social Confidence**. If your child becomes uncomfortable, she may be unwilling to put herself in that situation again, because she is afraid of being the center of attention.

That is why it's best to compliment your child quietly, if she lacks **Social Confidence**. Give her a high-five or a pat on the shoulder. But, don't draw any attention to her. Then, watch how she responds to your quiet praise. Another way to boost the confidence of your child, who lacks **Social Confidence**, is to acknowledge a group of children, who demonstrated good techniques, behaviors, or deeds. This helps build confidence in children by eliminating the pressure to perform.

Remember to identify why your child is afraid. Then, refrain from pushing her too hard in that direction. In other words, you'll want to use a different method of building your child up – one that yields positive results.

So, to answer the question posed at the beginning of this chapter – some children are naturally shy in unknown settings. Moreover, humans, in general, are naturally cautious in new environments. It's needed for survival and safety. *How can someone overcome that?* Well, you are in luck, because listed below are some of the techniques I use at *Hands of Life,* when I have a shy child in my class.

When I notice a child, who appears to be afraid to enter a room with other children (keep in mind these children probably don't know any of the other children), I encourage them to look around the room.

Then, I remind them that it's a "safe space," but that they don't have to go. I allow them to watch from the doorway for as long as they need to feel comfortable enough to enter the room. At this point, I'm just happy to get the children in the doorway, watching the other children. And, after a while, these shy children make their way into the room. Another technique I typically use with shy children involves their parents. If my shy students feel safer or more comfortable with their parents, I invite them to participate. This works especially well for my younger students.

It is important, however, that the parents don't try to convince or encourage their children to participate. *Why not?* Well, this may trigger performance anxiety in an already tricky situation. In other words, the more parents ask their children to participate, the more they will resist. In fact, parent often get frustrated or embarrassed by their children's shyness and resistance, which only makes them withdraw more. Therefore, it's best that parents quietly support their children, and refrain from making a big deal out of good behavior in public. You want your child to be confident and successful, but you also want her to have a safe experience.

Remember, the goal is for your child to leave with a new level of confidence, even if it's only an ounce. This applies to any new and positive environment. So, let the teacher or the instructor motivate your child and use their techniques to help him feel comfortable enough to participate.

The objective is to get your child close to the door, so she can see the environment. Allow her to observe the other children having fun and having a good time. Remind her that she is safe. Then, ask her questions like: *"Do you know any of the other children in the room?" "Are any of your friends from school here?"* And, if so, encourage her to talk to the child or children she knows..

Sometimes it helps, if a familiar face (i.e. a friend from school or relative) assists you. So, ask one of the "familiar" children to come over and talk to your child. Watch to see if the other child can get your child to participate. The truth is people; in general, feel more comfortable, when they see a familiar face. So, if your child knows another child there and she can see that that the other child is having fun, maybe, it will prompt your child to join in. *It's worth a try, right?*

On the flip side, if you child doesn't know anyone in the room, invite a few friendly children over and introduce yourself and your child. Ask the friendly children about themselves (i.e. what they like to do, hobbies, etc.) and try to find something that is relatable to your child. Then, suggest that the two children partner-up for the day. The great thing about this technique is it can work in any setting.

In a situation, where children are playing games, ask your child if she knows how to play the game. Then, ask her if she has played it before. And, if she says, "Yes," then say, "That's great!" Explain to her that the team needs another person to make it fair. If she still says, "No," then tell her how fun it is to play with more people. But, be careful not to pressure her to play, if she doesn't want to. Rather, give her the *option* to play. Keep in mind that if she doesn't know the rules, she may feel insecure about playing the game.

In addition, she may become hesitant to participate, because she has a **Social Fear** of the other children. Therefore, always make a mental checklist of things that may be preventing your shy child from taking the next step. *Is she just extremely shy or is she afraid of something specific?*

When I was in school, I remember some children standing outside of the gym, because they were afraid to play dodgeball. Once dodgeball ended, however, these children came inside. *Why didn't they go in originally?* Well, probably because they were shy. But once the thing that scared them was gone, they were fine. *So, how do you handle a situation, in which you child doesn't want to do something?* Well, you say, "Okay, that's fine, but why don't you play for a minute or two, and then you can sit out for the rest of time."

For something lice the dodgeball scenario, explain to your child that there's nothing to be afraid of with dodgeball, except that he may be eliminated from the game. Also, explain to him that it will help him develop new skills, conquer his fear of dodgeball, and build his **Physical Confidence**. Explain that there is a chance, he will get hit by the ball (but it won't hurt him). Then, encourage him to use his **Confidence of Will** to keep him playing. It's just a game.

If your child is still hesitant, try to point out a familiar face in the crowd – someone he knows. Remember; refrain from pushing your child into something he doesn't want to do. Then, listen to why your child doesn't want to go inside. If he has a sibling in the class, use them to entice your child to join in. Because, truth-be-told, it's easier for a sibling to entice a child, than you, the parent.

Ask your child's sibling to partner-up with him. Or, suggest that your child sit with you, and just watch the activity." Tell him that he can ask any questions he wants to ask. If you can do this, and your child is surrounded by a positive and strong support system, you'll have the tools to help your child overcome his lack of confidence, so he can step outside of his comfort zone.

But, just know that being shy is natural. *And, guess what?* Listed below are tips that you can use with your child to help him overcome his lack of confidence. If your child is shy around groups and he has signed up to do an activity, arrive at the venue early. *How do this help?* Well, your child will already be in place once the other children start arriving, so he won't have to walk into a room full of people. However, once the other children start arriving, back off and let the other children approach your child. Arriving late to a function can be intimidating to a child. Heck, it can be intimidating to adults too.

Think about it – going into a social setting where you don't know anyone. Not the greatest feeling for most people. So, you want to try to get your child to the venue first, if possible. Also, don't confuse shyness with simply not liking something – it is two separate things. An example of this involves the family of Maximus S., and more specifically, Maximus himself.

The Story of Maximus S. and His Persistent Parents

A boy named, Maximus, attended my martial arts school. When he first started attending my school, he was a combination of shy and strong-willed, and his parents were persistent, and did not give into the tactics he used to avoid coming to class. Because, I recognized his resistance, I recommend to his parents that they keep him out for a couple of months and then try again, but they weren't having any of that. Maximus' parents said that he was going to continue coming to class.

They stuck to their guns and Max came to class every week.

Maximus' parents' level of commitment is rare, especially when parents get resistance from their children. In fact, most parents don't have the time, energy, or patience to fight with their children on a daily or weekly basis. Eventually, however, Max realized he was going to come to class twice a week – no matter what, and by the 6th week, he was not only coming to class, but also participating without issue. He is still a student two years later! Moreover, his younger sister is also taking my class now.

Remember, if your child is very shy, support him. And, if you want him to do something, model what you want him to do. *Why?* Well, because there's a good chance he will copy what you are doing. So, if you have a young child, and you want him to participate in the class – do what the other children are doing – i.e. take off your shoes, take off your socks, sit down, and prepare for class. You child will eventually follow your lead. So, say to your child, "Hey how about I sit down first and then you do the same OR we can sit down together, if you'd like."

Whatever it takes to help your child feel confident and comfortable enough to participate or engage with other people, do it. You want your child to get to the point, where he understands that when Mom and Dad take him to a place, so he can participate in an activity, it's okay and he is safe. This will help your child overcome his **Social Fear.** And, the safer your child feels, the more he will open up and push past this fear. So, try this with your shy child, instead of getting frustrated with him or the situation. And, just remember, your child is shy for a reason. Maybe, he just can't help it.

Maybe, it's just natural for him. Teach your child that it's okay to enter new environments - provided they are safe and healthy.

Max used to cry and hide behind his parents' legs, when he had to do something that he didn't want to do in class.

Well, after a while his parents began coming into class with him. But, even then, he'd just sit on the side watching the other children. His mom would try to get him to participate, but he was a strong-willed child, who was a bit stubborn. He simply didn't want to do the exercise and that was that. So, after much thought, I suggested that his parents stop bringing Maximus to class until he was a little older. Well, his parents told me that they wouldn't stop bringing him, because he needed to boost his confidence and that they know this would be good for him.

Specifically his, **Physical Confidence**, **Social Confidence**, and **Confidence of Will**.

Now, it's rare that I see parents with this type of perseverance and conviction. So, Max's parents made him stick it out and keep coming. It is now two years later, and he's still my student. *And guess what?* He's phenomenal! He's super confident – physically, socially, and psychologically. He can now go into any class and perform – without fear. Now, Maximus is so much more confident than he was before. I mean like night-and-day and 100% different. And, his parents have been a big part of his transformation. So, stick to your guns, and be firm in your decision. Don't waver or back off, and do not let your child quit – anything, because persevering will build your child's confidence.

So, if you decide you want your child to do something, and you deem it important for him, make the decision, and stick to it. It will show him that he can work through challenges. Have your child say to himself, "Mom and Dad wouldn't make me go, if it wasn't going to be okay.

I have been asked many times by parents, if I thought their children would grow out of their shyness. And, sometimes these parents would share with me that they were also shy when they were children. Some would even tell that they're still shy to this day. So, they'd ask me, "Do you think my child can change?"

And, I'd answer, "Yes," every time. Yes, your child can change, but you need to teach her how to do it. Children pick up their parents' negative and positive traits. Therefore, the goal is to break the cycle of negative traits, so your child has fewer negative qualities than you. In other words, it's up to you to teach your child a different way of coping, thinking, and behaving. If you don't like something you've done in the past, or a certain trait you possess, then do whatever it takes to help your child avoid exhibiting that trait.

And, if you don't feel confident, as an adult, then put in place as many strategies, as possible, to help your child become more confident. Because, if you truly want your child to be different, you'll need to expose her to as many environments, as you can, so she can learn to defeat unwanted, inherited behaviors. However, she may still start out just like you, because she is part you. But, if she begins to show certain traits, do something to change them.

And, once you start down the path of helping your child change, you'll have the confidence to stick to your guns. And, if you enroll your child in something that will help her confidence, you'll reap the benefits - just like the family of Maximus.

CHAPTER EIGHT

How Can I Build More Confidence in My Child?

"Think like a queen. A queen is not afraid to fail. Failure is just another stepping stone to greatness."

~Oprah

There are many ways to build confidence. The first thing you should do is identify the type of confidence that needs to be boosted. Once you have identified which one needs attention, start taking baby steps to build it up. Building confidence, for the most part, means overcoming some type of fear. In short, identify the fear, learn about it, take steps and build up the courage needed to beat the fear and increase confidence.

Listed below are formulas, diagrams, worksheets, and tools that can help with the building process:

- **The Confidence-Building Perseverance Cycle**

- **The 6 Steps to Overcoming Fear Building Confidence**

- **The 6 Steps to Facing Your Failures and Mistakes**

Every fear has certain characteristics attached to it. For example, being afraid of the dark is what I consider, **Misplaced Fear**. It's when you have a real fear, but allow it to appear, when it's not truly needed. Your child shouldn't be afraid of the dark, unless there is a reason to be afraid of the dark like he is lost in the woods at night, or he witnessed something traumatic at night. But, your child's eyes cannot see well in the dark, so he is, in a sense, vulnerable at night. So, his brain signals that he should be afraid.

So, help your child build more confidence by coaching and guiding him through his failures, mistakes, and fears. And, as you probably know from experience, your child will get through his failures, fears, and mistakes, if he has confidence. So, help your child identify his failures, mistakes, and fears, and teach him how to overcome them, why he needs to overcome them, and why they are necessary for personal growth.

Because, failure, fear, and mistakes are necessary. It is important to note that if your child doesn't aspire to go to the next level of skill and understanding, there will be no need for him to make mistakes. I mean, your child can take the safe route and just be timid and average. And, if he is lucky, maybe he can still be super successful, as an adult. BUT the odds are against that. In fact, those, who make the least mistakes and find solutions to problems, are not only highly successful, but also have fewer regrets.

On the other hand, if you want you want your child to be a great student, baseball player, athlete, or entrepreneur, then he needs to make mistakes. So, to build your child's confidence, you will need to guide him through his fears, mistakes, and failures. Remember, how I talked a lot about fears in the last chapter, well in this chapter, I'm going to talk about failures and mistakes. *"The seeds to greatness and success are in failure."* Failure also includes mistakes. If you want your child to be great or improve, he will have to make mistakes and fail, from time-to-time. When your child fails or makes mistakes, he learns what his weaknesses are. And, when he knows his weaknesses, he has the power to improve.

So, if you could identify and strengthen your child's weakness until it was strong, could you do it, or would you collapse under the pressure? In other words, when you fix a piece of something that failed, that one piece of the whole is strengthened with the expectation that it will not fail again. That piece is taken care of, even though; a completely different weakness may pop up and fail. *Regardless, when something falls short, you strengthen that area.*

Therefore, teach your child that it's absolutely fine if she makes a mistake, or is not good at something on the first try. For example, say you are teaching your child how to tie her shoes. You provide her with positive feedback or PCP (Praise-Correct-Praise) by saying, "Hey, you're

doing great. I love how you're getting the first part down, but when
you make bunny ears, I know something's happening, can you tell me
what's happening?" Pinpoint where
the mistake is occurring, and, if your
child becomes frustrated or discouraged, video-record what's causing
the frustration.

Video-recording your child's
reaction helps her see the mistake.
It's impossible to perform an activity
with 100% focus and watch yourself
at the same time. It's also difficult to
be aware of your own mistakes. That
is why video-recording is an awesome learning tool.

Coach your child through the
mistakes, provided she has at least
a small amount of healthy confidence. If your child still doesn't understand what you're telling her,
video-record the mistake and watch
the footage with her. Say, "Look at
this bunny ear right there on the

video. It's a good one, but it is a little big. It's nice and long, but it needs to be shorter. If you make it shorter, it will give you more room to pull and tighten them."

So, identify the mistake or failure. *What do you think caused this to be unsuccessful?* Then, point it out to your child, from a video, drawing, or diagram. After that, teach her how to fix the mistake. Now, it is important to point out that your child may still be in her head and upset and frustrated. Your job, therefore, is to get her past the emotional part, so she can process the lesson. Share a personal story about a time when you had a failure or made a mistake – how did you fix it? For example, you could say," I had trouble doing this_____ when I was your age. And, just recently, I had trouble learning how to do something new on my computer." Let your child know you're not perfect either, and that you also make mistakes and fail sometimes.

Because, honestly, most children view their parents as superheroes or perfect people, who never make mistakes or fail. For example, say to her, "I know you think I'm the best or strongest guy or girl in the world, but the truth is there have been times when other people were way stronger/better/smarter than me. I had to put in extra time and work a little harder to "measure up" to the people around me." *See how I did that?* So, constantly reinforce the idea that it is okay to make mistakes and fail from time-to-time, and let your child know that with confidence, she can work through mistakes and failures and find her path to improvement.

It is important to support your child, as he navigates through the trials and tribulations of life. *What is the best way to do that?* Well, by helping him identify what is preventing him from getting back up and continuing. *What is the fear?* You may want to use the Praise-Correct-Praise method to ensure that you don't accidentally lower your child's confidence. You don't want him to stop listening to you, because he is so overwhelmed that it's impossible for him to understand the lesson you are trying to teach him.

For example, you could say something like this, "I just want you to know that you're doing awesome! But, I noticed that you are struggling a little in this area. Let's video-record what's happening and try to pinpoint the mistake. Oh, I see it; it looks like something is happening with one of the bunny ears that you are making with your shoestrings. How about I show you how I would do the bunny ear and you can copy me?" If you do this, you child will be able to see with his own eyes what he is doing wrong. As a result, he will be able to correct the mistake. This will also teach him how to self-correct and analyze his mistakes and failures, which is fantastic.

That's how you can guide and support your child through his failures and mistakes. Because, really, you don't want your child to carry mistakes and failure with him and you don't want to do everything for your child. **Note:** Regarding tying shoes, you may want to start this process around four-years-old. *Why?* Well, it's a lot easier to teach your child how to tie his shoes at four, than at six or seven-years-old.

Coaches and teachers also use tools like nurturing, guidance, and support to help build confidence in children. So, use these tools to help your child overcome obstacles, fears, failures, and mistakes. And, keep emboldening your child to do new things. Encourage him to try new things and think outside-of-the-box. If you see your child trying to do something – anything productive, praise him for the effort. BUT, don't tell him that he is "perfect" or you may inflate his ego.

You also don't want to build up **False Confidence** or encourage arrogance or cockiness. So, say something like, "You're doing fantastic! I see you're really improving and making progress. When you put time into practicing, I see the effort." This type of support strengthens confidence. It's like watering a flower of confidence. But, no matter what you do, don't lie to your child.

In other words, don't instill **False Confidence** in your child. Be honest. If you lie to your child, she may develop a **False Confidence** that's not real or accurate. For example, if your co-worker is performing a task poorly and you tell her that she is doing fantastic, you are instilling **False Confidence** in her, if it's not warranted. This type of confidence can be detrimental to a child, who is shy or insecure. So, always tell your child the truth – if he is weak in an area, that's okay, just guide and support him through it.

In self-defense class, if a teacher grabs a child by the wrist and tells her to escape, most times, the child doesn't really "escape." No, in reality, the teacher just releases the child, and as a result, she develops a **False Confidence** in the child. *Why is **False Confidence** a problem?* Well, when a child grabs and pins another child with the **False Confidence**, the child with the false sense of confidence becomes devastated when she learns that she is not as skilled, as she previously thought, which leads to an even lower self-confidence.

Therefore, you don't want to build **False Confidence** in your child. Rather, develop and strengthen confidence in your child. So, if I grab a child by the arm, and hold it firmly, but not with my strongest grip, she will probably be able to wiggle free. But, if I grab that same child with my strongest grip and she is just now learning, she is probably not going to be able to wiggle free.

It's impossible. There's no way she could wiggle free, because she doesn't know what she is doing. According to Oprah Winfrey, it's important to pass confidence down to children. It's important to teach your child how to embrace failure and use it to learn a valuable lesson that will help her succeed in the future.

CHAPTER NINE

What Role Does a School Teacher Play
in the Life of a Child?

"Don't you dare, for one more second,
surround yourself with people, who are not
aware of the greatness that you are."

~Jo Blackwell-Preston

Truth-be-told, school teachers have a tough job. They spend 6-hours, per day with your children, which is more than most people spend with their children. You are responsible for your child, but many times, the school system's hands are tied and there are restrictions on what administrators can say, teach, and do. Some teachers are awesome, especially the ones that model success, motivation, and confidence, and understand the mindset of human beings.

Teachers often have many students, who don't believe in themselves, lack confidence, have a hard time completing tasks, and are not very communicative. You can see it in their work, but you may not see the social side of things. For example, a child comes back from recess feeling down or sad, but refuses to tell you why he is feeling that way, well, the best thing you can do in this situation is to be "available" and present for him. Also, look at the problem from a triangle perspective. This triangle should comprise three different focuses: manners, courtesy, and confidence.

But, guess what? You can really boost your child's by teaching her how to be respectful, courteous and motivated, and by providing her with the tools, exercises, and drills she needs to overcome hurdles like mistakes and failures. *What's the best way to do that?* Well, by making the process of making mistakes and failing *fun*. *Fun?* Yes, fun. And, teaching your child that it's okay to *not* be perfect. Therefore, the key to boosting your child's confidence is reinforcing this mindset.

It bears noting that even though parents and teachers try to reinforce children and build their confidences, sometimes the focus is lost. In other words, other things pop up that take precedence over building confidence. But, even if parents did focus solely on building confidence and prompting a positive mindset, centered on respect, courtesy, and motivation, most children would still resist. But, keep trying anyways. Plant the seed (your child), water it, and cultivate it.

Oh, and don't forget, your outer triangle aka "village" of friends, coaches, extended family, and neighbors. Develop a shared mindset with the people in *your* support system. Craft goals for your child – goals that he can achieve. But, most of all, adopt a "village mentality." To boost your child's confidence, you will need the help of others in your child's inner circle. The only way your child's confidence level will increase is if he has a strong support system surrounding him.

In other words, surround your child with friends and families, who share your values. *How can you tell if they share your same values?* Well, by asking them what they think about certain life and child-rearing topics. Once, you have a good idea of the people, who share your mindset, work together to look out for each other's children. Another thing you can do to boost your child's confidence is to direct him towards the elders in your community. For example, you could allow someone like Mr. Bell from my old neighborhood share his wisdom with your child. As you recall, Mr. Bell was the wise old man that lived in my grandmother's neighborhood. He was also the person, who taught me and my friends valuable life lessons. I can't stress enough how important it is to have a "village mentality."

I want to point out one more time just how important teachers are when it comes to building confidence in children. Teachers are responsible for preparing students for a life outside of school. In other words, teachers teach children how to read, write, analyze, research, etc., so they can eventually go to college, graduate, and enter the workforce. Children, who can read, write, and speak well tend to be more confident than those who can't do those things. Being prepared for life, a sport, a job and so on, helps a person feel more confident. So, teachers, in a sense, are at the forefront of building your child's confidence. Without them, we would have a lot of insecure and unsuccessful adults.

But, you play a big part in building your child's confidence also, along with coaches and martial arts instructors like me. We all work together to instill in children confidence and important values. Coaches and martial art instructors instill honor, respect, and teamwork in them. We also teach them skills that boost their **Physical Confidence** and **Confidence of Will**. So, as you can see this "village" is critical for your child's self-esteem and success.

The *Super Confidence Academy* was designed to help you teach your child confidence. It is an academy that teaches confidence. We, the instructors, are responsible for instilling in your child a higher self-esteem and self-confidence. *So, can adults also use this material to improve their self-confidence?* YES! You can easily apply the concepts and exercises found in this book to adults. The purpose of this book is to provide you with insight on how to develop, maintain, and/or rebuild confidence – for your child and yourself.

CHAPTER TEN

From Super Shy to Super Confident!

Is it Possible? Is it Necessary?

"Self-confidence is the memory of success."

~David Storey

Can a person, who is extremely shy, become extremely confident? Yes! In fact, shy people can transform themselves and become confident individuals. Now, that doesn't mean extremely shy people will magically transform into outgoing, extroverted, life-of-the-party people. *Why not?* Well, because, some traits are intrinsic or genetic. They are a natural part of what makes you who you are. Those traits can be altered – with effort, but they stay with you forever. However, a person, who is quiet and soft-spoken, CAN become confident – with effort.

In other words, a person can become less shy – if she tries. Being a *shy person* is different from being a *quiet person*. A shy person tends to be afraid of interacting with or speaking in groups. A quiet person, on the other hand, may just be laid-back and mellow, by nature. Just because someone's quiet doesn't mean she lacks confidence.

My friend, Mark, is super mellow, laid-back, and quiet. BUT, he's not a shy person, even though he may appear that way. No, he's confident – just quiet until you get to know him. But, once he gets to know you, he's more talkative and outgoing. It just takes time for him to get to know people. Listed below is an example of how a person can be quiet and still be confident.

Anna B.

Anna B. is quiet. She is also very soft-spoken and reserved. And, ironically, when Anna first started my class, she didn't like to speak in front of others. She also didn't like to be praised in front of the other students. In addition, Anna tended to shun kata performances and sparring matches, because she didn't like aggressive activities. Anna is not athletically explosive, and she's not very muscular. Moreover, she's a sensitive person. In other words, she's kind, polite, and she has impeccable manners.

In Traditional Chinese Medicine this personality type is described as "Yin" or "Yin-Yin." Well, after working with Anna B. for years, I decided to motivate her, in a supportive way, to expend more energy, generate more power, and give more of an effort. I just couldn't understand why, after all of these years, she had little-to-no energy. In fact, I would often ask myself, "Why doesn't Annabelle put any "oomph "into her technique?" She wouldn't kiai (spirit yell) loud or use her voice. It was like she wasn't even trying.

I tried all different techniques to inspire, motivate, and encourage her, but nothing was helping. And, in the beginning when I tried to give her tips and corrections (using classic motivational teaching techniques), she would just cry. Exasperated, I started to pay close attention to what I said to her and how I said it.

After I changed how I communicated with Anna, her confidence and energy improved. She also started to listen to me more. It was important for me to address her confidence issue with care. I didn't want to cause it to dip even further. But, what I didn't realize was that Anna was doing her best. You see, because of the nature of her personality and body type, her best effort was hard to see. I mean, even her parents didn't think she was giving 100%.

Well, one New Year's Eve, another family from my school, *Hands of Life Martial Arts*, had a party at their house with many families from school. While at the party, I observed Annabelle and some of my other students, playing. In this casual setting, Anna laughed loudly, talked continuously, and moved like the Energizer Bunny! Her energy level was off the charts! So, the next time she was on the mat, I reminded her of when she played with her friends at the New Year's Eve party. I said to her, "Anna, come on - I've seen you play with your friends, so

I know you have the speed and power to successful train."

So, that day I had the class do some speed contests to see, who could punch the fastest. This time I noticed that Annabelle was repeatedly coming in first for speed. She was also fast with her hands. The strange thing is she didn't appear to be moving especially fast or displaying the energy I saw at the party. She wasn't explosive, when she was alone, and she wasn't fast, when standing next to someone else either, but if she was around a group of children, she was a dynamo! She had found a way to be fast through an efficiency of motion. Ironically, Annab was able to do this, because she didn't have the muscle mass to impede her movement. As a result, it made her faster than everyone else. She had fun with the drill that day and was successful at it! Yet, it still didn't match her energy from the party. The interesting part was she could do a variety of skills and techniques that increased her speed.

In fact, once while at a tournament, Anna sparred with the other children in her age and belt level group. By this time, she was a Brown Belt. We were a tad bit worried that she would get nervous and be outmatched. She had a blank look on her face – the one I mistakenly associated with her not giving enough effort. So, naturally, I wanted to give her a pep talk to prepare her for the matches. I said, "Anna, just do what you do in class. When the opponent comes in, cover and counter, as fast as you can, just like you did with the speed drills in class."

Well, Anna B.'s first match started, and what happened was amazing! The opponent rushed in to hit her, and she used her speed to fire her hands off. Then, her opponent ran right into her fist - with his face! You're not supposed to make contact to the face, but even the judge knew it was unintentional. Anna's opponent came in so fast and she literally punched him in the face, before he could even move forward. It was amazing to see her hold her own against her opponent! She was so confident, and I was so proud of her!

After the tournament, I realized something profound - just because she had fun and acted "free" at the New

Year's party didn't mean she would exhibit the same energy, when concentrating or focusing on something else. In other words, the intensity of her energy could be equivalent to her output, but different in appearance. So, if I had only concentrated on a specific marker of Anna's speed or power, I probably would have missed it, because it was delivered differently than I thought it should be.

So, is Anna now going to be this super muscular, explosive, powerful, loud, and over-the-top, extroverted person? Maybe, it's possible, but not probable. That's not who Anna B. is naturally.

However, the point of this story is to demonstrate how a shy individual can transform themselves into a confident person, while maintaining her natural personality. Anna didn't become a different person, but she did improve her confidence level in a variety of areas.

At the beginning, she was terrified, scared, quiet, and tearful when she was corrected or encouraged to put forth more effort. Not anymore! Now, she faces her opponents, performs, weapons forms, kata, and she confidently speaks in front of groups, leads our class in warm-ups, and even willingly answers questions in class. Remember, you can't transform your child's personality, but you can help make them to become more confident. They don't have to change or alter their personality to change their confidence level.

All your child has to do is be open to change. If he or she can do that, they will experience a newfound self-confidence in areas that were weak before.

So, can your child transform from super shy to super confidence? YES! Just accept that even when, not if, your child becomes super confident, they still will not have an extroverted, outgoing rock-star personality, because that is not who they are. Make sure not to confuse a high energy, extroverted personality (who has confidence) with an introverted, reclusive personality (who lacks confidence). *Why not?* Well, because that's like comparing apples to oranges - they are just different.

CHAPTER ELEVEN

What Can Lower Confidence or
Take It Away?

"No one can make you feel inferior without
your consent."

~Eleanor Roosevelt

What takes a child's confidence away? Well, confidence can be stripped or diminished due to a variety of situations. The good thing, however, is it can be rebuilt. *So, what can lower or take away my child's self-esteem and confidence?* Criticism and negative feedback and input from you, teachers, and coaches can damage a child's confidence. Moreover, unhealthy or stressful relationships can also play a role in lowering confidence. *How does this hurt confidence?* Well, these factors can have an indirect effect on it. For example, say your child receives criticism from a coach or teacher, who doesn't really understand the mindset of a child or consider the impact that words have on a specific child. Not all people, who work with children, are equal, and not all of them are able to connect with children the same way.

In fact, many coaches are Dads, who volunteer their time. So, because they are not teachers and not required to take coaching classes or learn how children learn best, they may or may not be able to help build a child's confidence. Some teachers and coaches are not nice and simply don't want to take the time to sharpen or improve their skills. There are even some teachers and coaches, who are mean to certain students and players, because they don't like them, or they aren't as skilled as other players. Unfortunately, some of them have "favorites."

As a professional martial arts instructor and parent, I think coaches, teachers and martial arts instructors should treat all children like they're their own children. They should not have "favorites." I don't have a favorite out of my two boys. There may be things that one of my sons does that I don't like and there may be things that the other one does that I don't like, but I would never pick one over the other, or choose a favorite. I try to treat them both equally. Now, sometimes I may take different a different approach with each of them, but I don't favor one over the other. Or, dislike or love one more than the other.

The same goes for my students. I don't favor some students over others. And, I try to treat all of them with an equal amount of respect and compassion. And, although some students require more attention than others, due to issues like a lack of discipline, a lack of focus, issues with licensing, physical challenges, or even a lack of confidence, I still view them the same as my other students. That's why parents bring their children to my school – because I treat their children with respect and fairness. Listed below is a story that highlights the importance of treating all children with respect and fairness.

J.G.

When I was in seventh grade, J.G., moved to our town from a small city. The family moved to my town because J.G.'s older brother had become involved with the wrong crowd and gotten in trouble. Frightened for her older son's welfare, their mother moved to a new location. Well, from the moment I met J.G., I knew we were going to be good friends. I knew that being the "new kid" in town could be rough, so I befriended him. Eventually, I found out that J.G. was from Puerto Rico, and had recently moved from a predominately white town with little diversity. Since I was the child of an African American father and Caucasian mother, it didn't matter to me what J.G.'s race or skin color was. We became fast friends and are still close to this very day.

Well, one day, when I was in seventh grade, J.G.'s mom walked up to me, while I was standing outside of school, waiting to be picked up and said," I don't want you hanging out with my son anymore." We were 12-years-old at the time, which is way too young for an adult to approach a child like that, in my opinion. *To my knowledge, we hadn't done anything wrong and we hadn't got-*

ten in trouble, so why was she coming at me like that? She then said, "We moved from Elizabeth to get away from people like *you*, so please stay away from J.G."

J.G.'s mom chastised me in front of the other students, which was embarrassing. I can still remember the look on the faces of my friends and classmates. J.G. was there when his mom criticized me, but he didn't say anything. But, what could he say, his mom was in charge. It was hurtful, but I brushed it off, and pretended not to care. Still, I couldn't stop thinking about what she said. I remember thinking to myself, "What did I do wrong? I didn't do anything wrong." The only conclusion I could come to was that J.G.'s mom was crazy.

Don't get me wrong this wasn't the first time I had been discriminated against. But, this time it was different because J.G. was my friend and it appeared that his mom didn't like me simply because of my race. I was baffled because J.G., his brother, and his mother were all Puerto Rican, which is considered a minority. J.G.'s mom didn't want her son hanging around me because I was Black. I later learned that the "boys" that J.G. used to get in trouble with were also Black, so his mom decided lump us all together, even though we were separate individuals.

I knew I wasn't a thug or criminal, and I wasn't roaming around town getting in trouble with her older son, but it was still distressing to know that that's how she viewed me. It didn't take me long to figure out that it was all about my skin tone and race. She didn't want J.G. hanging out with *any* "Black kids," regardless of their characters or personalities. She *only* wanted J.G. and his older brother to be friends with "White kids." Truthfully, that was a tough experience for me – one that initially lowered my confidence and self-esteem, but later made me stronger, as person.

So, as you can see a variety of situations can strip your child's confidence. But, if I had to guess, I'd say approximately 99% of these situations involve other people. So, once again, that's why it's important to adopt a "village mindset." It's important that you communicate with your child's coaches and teachers. I know you probably don't want to be annoying or a pain-in-the-butt to these mentors, but you need them. Talk to them about the things that are important to you and work with them to do what's best for your child. Also, let them know that you welcome feedback, advice, support, and suggestions.

Social situations can also damage your child's confidence. In fact, social situations where your child is excluded from activities, made fun of because of his clothes, hair, or something he does not do well like not being able to ride a bike without training wheels, or not being able to tie his shoes can cause his confidence to drop. *Why?* Because these social situations test your child's confidence. The key to conquering his lack of **Social Confidence** is to listen to him when he tells you about things that have happened to him around other children. Listen and be open, available, and calm. Also, be supportive and always keep an "open door policy" with him.

But, keep in mind, that your child may wait a while and then ask you a question out of the blue, like a week or month later. She may say something like, "Do you like my hair, Mommy?" And, your response should be, "Yes, of course I do! I love your hair. Why do you ask?" Then, she may say something like, "Well, one of my classmates told me that she didn't like my hair." Then, you should ask, "When was this?" She may reply with something like, "About two months ago."

So, as you can see, your child could be holding in something that happened to her for weeks or months, before sharing her thoughts with you. Think about it, she could be sitting on a question or conflicting feelings for 8 weeks or longer! Yikes! The good news is that most times, your child will eventually come to you with her questions and doubts.

Suppressing feelings and emotions can have a negative effect on your child's confidence! Thankfully, however, there are signs to low self-esteem and poor confidence, so pay attention to them. If the people in your child's life can catch the changes in him, then it's easy to get his confidence back on track. These types of situations are exercises in confidence-building. Remember, if your child appears to be insecure or "down and out," his confidence may be in a state of flux. Thus, to repair his confidence, he needs you to reassure him that he is handsome, and there is nothing wrong him. Explain to your child that the reason he is so awesome is because she resembles you and his Daddy.

It really is important that your child feel confidence in every aspect of his life – always. If he is confident, he can brush-off those, who are critical or jealous of him. Keep in mind though, that your child is always listening, so he may overhear you complimenting another child, as a result, he may become envious of the attention the other child is receiving. Maybe, he heard you say to another child that he had awesome curls, and then became jealous of the other child's curls – and the attention you gave him.

Yes, you complimented another child, but that doesn't mean you don't think your child's hair is just as fabulous, because you do. Still, to your child it means you love the other child more or you think the other child is "better," than him, because you complimented him. As a result, he begins to lack confidence in himself. *What happens next?* Well, your child deliberately tries to make the other child feel bad about himself, so he can feel better. Don't get me wrong, he can't help how he feels, BUT he doesn't have to act on those feelings, especially if they are negative and will hurt someone else.

Therefore, the sooner you apply the strategies for **Overcoming Fears** or **Overcoming Failures and Mistakes**, the sooner child can banish his doubts, fears, and insecurities and become more confident. The aim is to make your child bulletproof from insults and criticisms. But, developing a strong confidence takes time. It's like forging steel. It's a process that has to be placed under extreme heat, and then hit repeatedly to remove any weaknesses. Therefore, in this situation, it is about allowing your child to face the harshest conditions, so he can grow.

Weaknesses are just opportunities to become better or stronger. Remember, the concepts in this book can also apply to adults. For example, a sales rep may be afraid to approach customers in the store, so she eventually leaves her job, because she can't take the stress. Well, if you are in a similar situation, don't fret because this guide can teach you how to better manage your stress, overcome your fear AND boost your confidence.

I used to be a sales rep and it was pretty stressful. I preferred being in the store over cold-calling customers. I didn't like phone sales, because customers always knew that I was calling about an order, or to check-on payments. I was also required to upsell additional products to them, if I could.

My preference was to work in the store and help customers, because I didn't have to upsell products, as often. *Was it my lack of confidence?* Maybe... I didn't want to be rejected. More so, it just didn't feel genuine. And, eventually, it dawned on me that I enjoyed personal interactions. Talking to customers over the phone didn't provide me with the connections I wanted. Plus, I felt like a failure, when I couldn't upsell to customers. *And, when a person feels like a failure, guess what happens?* Well, her confidence declines.

159

Even coaches, who yell or scream at their players, can lower your child's confidence. Believe it or not, that approach is tough on a child. So, the best way to handle this situation is to say something like, "Go out there and try your best, work hard, and your coach will appreciate the effort." It's important to note that most coaches are "yellers." And, they don't just yell negative things to players; they also yell positive things like, "Good job!" It's just their way of communicating. Therefore, the best thing you can do is just keep encouraging and supporting your child.

Rejection can come in many forms, but almost every time it damages a person's confidence level. For example, say a teen boy wants to ask a classmate to the school dance, but she says, "No." Well, just because she refused to go to the dance with him, doesn't necessarily mean she's not interested in him. Maybe, she doesn't want to go to the dance because she has other plans, or maybe, she promised to go with someone else, or maybe, she doesn't like parties and dances at all. There are a thousand different reasons why she may have told him, "No." But, in his mind, she rejected him, which hurts like crazy. And, because of this rejection, his self-esteem plummeted. *But guess what?* His confidence quickly rebounded and he kept trying to score that first date.

The truth is, lots of people, who tried to date their future spouses for weeks, months, or even years, before they agreed to that first date. *How did they do it?* Well, through perseverance and commitment. They eventually began dating and then married! Now, they have 2 kids, house, and a dog. Although, the teen boy didn't get to go with his dream girl to the dance, she did later agree to go out on a date with him. And, now they are happily married with a baby on the way. So, ultimately, it was his perseverance and will, along with a healthy dose of confidence thrown in for good measure that helped him snag his dream girl.

However, trying obsessively to make something that's not going to happen, happen is the mere definition of *insanity*. In fact, the definition of insanity is doing the same thing repeatedly and expecting different results. So, *discour-*

age your child from doing that. Still, there are situations where doing the same thing repeatedly can yield different results. Regardless, protect your child's confidence by teaching her how to properly gauge the situation. But, if the signs are good, encourage her to continue trying until she makes progress.

Did you know that people, who are persistent can sense change in others? Well, they can! But, if a child lacks confidence, he'll keep repeating the same mistakes. A confident person, on the other hand, senses that something is not working and moves. **Confidence of Creation** refers to doing something new – i.e. making something, drawing a picture, or starting a business. But, it is important to understand that if your child has poor confidence and his creation doesn't turn out like he had hoped or envisioned, he may experience a dip in confidence.

For instance, look at the Wall Street tycoons. When the stock-market crashed, some of them went to extreme levels. Their confidences also went way down. Some even committed suicide! But, you can't allow your child to give up hope, because it will destroy his confidence. *What should you do?* Start rebuilding your child's confidence - from scratch. You did it before, you can do it again.

Your child may also lose her confidence, when faced with certain situations. For example, your child draws something, but then deems someone else's artwork "better," she may begin to doubt her own artistic abilities, which lowers her confidence. Therefore, the key is to encourage her to *not* compare herself to others. Teach your child to be inspired, not envious, of the accomplishments and skills of others. Motivate her, and encourage her to ask, "How?" *How did she get so good at this or that, or how did she develop those skills?* Teach your child how to look at her work, identify weak areas, and improve them. And, once your child finds something that inspires her, encourage her to go for it!

If your child is motivated by other children or situations, inspire him to put his best foot forward. But, if your child compares himself to others −constantly pointing how much better the other children are, then it will eventually zap his confidence. This is what I call **Catabolic Confidence**. **Catabolic Confidence** is when someone sabotages his confidence by self-doubting and comparing himself to others. So, if you want your child to do better, the best thing you can do for him is suggest that he study someone, who is good at the sport, academic subject, or activity, and practice it repetitively. Encourage your child to emulate what he saw and learned until he acquires the confidence and skills needed to be successful.

Don't, however, encourage your child to be someone, he is not. For instance, don't try to make your child into Michael Jordan, because there can only be one Michael Jordon, rather inspire him to watch basketball games featuring Michael Jordan, with the goal of learning his moves, practicing, and developing a plan/steps that can help your child achieve Michael Jordan's level of athletic greatness. In other words, help your child figure out how to "fake someone out" on the court or "shake someone" on the football field. Also, help your child figure out how to dribble between his legs to get around a "defender." Explain to your child that the more he practices, the more confident in his skills, he will become. Thus, embolden your child to learn the basic skills of the sport from a coach, and practice until he finds his own natural rhythm.

Because, the simple truth is your child learns just from watching others. And, although, at the beginning, he is just "copying" another person's style, eventually with training and coaching, he will find his own way. More specifically, he will take bits and pieces of what he learned and create his own style. And, as a result, he will gain confidence in a variety of areas.

CHAPTER TWELVE

The Fear of Making Mistakes and
Trying New Things

"Each time we face our fear, we gain strength, courage, and confidence."

~Theodore Roosevelt

As mentioned in previous chapters, fear is a natural thing. It's your body's first-line of self-defense. So, when you are scared, there's usually a reason for your fear. Well, the same thing can be said of your child. For instance, if I'm afraid to go into a dark room, there's a reason for that. Most of the time, this type of fear is misplaced, meaning it's not based on reality.

But, if I'm afraid to do a front flip or a physical activity, where I could be in-jured hurt, then that's a real fear. I could get hurt doing it. So, to combat this very real fear, I perform the four "Ps": preparation, patience, perseverance, and practice. I prepare myself to do the activity or task, and then I go through the stages, from the bottom – up. So, if I want to learn how to do a front flip in the air with no springboard or trampoline, I understand that I need to be strong enough to support myself. And, I do that by watching others and learning how to do the flips – with confidence. I may start with floor tumbling and rolls until I feel more comfortable doing a rotation in the air. Remember, everything happens in steps. *It's a process.*

So, now that you have a better understanding of how fear and confidence are intertwined, how can you get your child past her fear of making mistakes, so she can try new things? Well, in previous chapters, I discussed guiding and supporting your child through her mistakes and failures, and teaching her that failures and mistakes are simply seeds of success. Well, I suggest that you explain to her that the only way she can improve and boost her confidence is by identifying her strengths and weaknesses, practicing daily, and exerting extra effort towards being successful.

Give your child an analogy that centers on the premise that even if it isn't broken, she can still make it better. For example, ask your child to imagine that she came across a bike with obvious flaws – it has two flat tires, a broken headlight, AND a missing fender. Then, ask her this, "If you saw this bike could you immediately pinpoint what needed to be fixed? Would the bike function better, if these things were fixed?" Next, ask your child to identify the broken parts, and explain why these parts are like mistakes. Lastly, explain to your child that if these parts aren't fixed, someone else will point them out and the owner of the bike could get in big trouble for riding around on a bike that is faulty.

You may also want to use a house analogy. *Ask your child to explain to what happens, when someone makes a mistake on the foundation of a house she is building? What happens to the house?* Use imagery to help her wrap her mind around the notion that everyone makes mistakes, and it's okay. Explain to her that it's even better, when someone else recognizes them for you, because then you can fix them, so they won't become a problem later. Tell your child that it's only going to make her better and more confident in the long-run.

And, once you can get your child past her fear of making mistakes, then your job is to offer guidance and support by telling her that it's okay. You could say something like, "Embrace your mistakes. Don't make them on purpose, but when you do make them, be grateful that someone, like me, a coach, a teacher, a friend, a martial arts instructor, or even a stranger pointed them out to you. We are only trying to help you, so you don't keep making the same mistakes repeatedly, leading to low confidence and a poor self-esteem." Then, have your child ask herself the following questions, "Is there anything I could improve or fix?"

And, if your child tells you that she is afraid of something, increase her confidence and banish the fear simply saying to her, "Well, that's okay! Everyone makes mistakes. What do you think will happen if you mess up? I promise you that no harm will come to you, if you make a mistake or fail at something." If she tells you that she is afraid that she will not be as good as the other children. Then, validate her feelings and reply with, "Okay, I get that. But, here's the thing, it doesn't really matter what they think. You can't worry about them. You can only do your best. But, guess what? I bet the other children will respect you for giving it your all. They may even copy you! So, you can either be a leader or a follower. I'd personally prefer to be a leader – a trendsetter. But, the thing is, you may have to muster up your inner courage and confidence to do it. Do you have it in you?"

You can also instill confidence in your child by giving him some independence. Allow him to be his best by teaching him how to say to himself, "I can do this. I am a lot stronger than people think. I'll be okay just as long as I keep practicing."

Wait...but what if your child has a fear of trying new foods, what can you do to get him past this fear? Truth-be-told, this is a tricky one, because all children have things they like to eat and things they wouldn't touch with a 10-foot pole. If your child refuses to eat certain foods like fruits and veggies, develop a system, where he can "earn" the foods he likes simply by trying a new food. Now, the key to making this technique work is being creative and coming up with a variety of foods, while still giving him a choice. But, whatever you do, don't force him to eat one specific fruit or veggie.

Rather, offer him a variety of foods to see which ones he will eat. Start with two or three, and then introduce new ones on rotation. It's tricky, so you may have to combine the new foods with the old ones that he likes. If it's a textural thing, change the texture of the food by whipping it, blending it, or preparing it differently. Do whatever it takes to get your child to try something new.

What about a reward system? Well, a reward system is always beneficial when trying to get a child to try something new and different. BUT, you don't want to always rely on this system, because it can create **False Confidence**. The truth is, life doesn't always have rewards, so the real reward must come from within – trying something and being successful at it. The reward is the new experience – learning more and expanding his mind.

Also, reward your child with things he would have had anyways. For instance, say, "I know you love chicken nuggets, so when you eat the fish on your plate or this healthy meal, you can have chicken nuggets for the next meal, or if you eat healthy for two days, you can have chicken nuggets on Friday." The key to helping your child move past her fear of trying new things is to make the new things fun and challenging. If it's entertaining enough, your child will eventually have the confidence to participate.

Also, if you want your child to do something, start by doing it yourself. In other words, if your child sees you or her siblings doing something, she will most likely want to do it too, especially if you all appear to be having a good time. That's how you get her over the fear of making mistakes and trying new things.

Truth-be-told, I've done this with other people's children hundreds of times. Now, with your own child, it's always a little bit more challenging, but I've done it with my own children, as well. The key is getting out of your own way. Don't try to do everything by yourself. In other words, don't forget about your "virtual village." Allow your "village members" to teach your child valuable life lessons AND reinforce the lessons you teach at home. It will only make things easier for you in the long-run.

CHAPTER THIRTEEN

Using the Power of Voice and Learning to Speak Up!

"Life is 10% of what you experience, and 90% of how you respond to it."

~Dorothy M. Neddermeyer

Because most people are afraid of public speaking, try to avoid confrontations, and just don't like expressing their feelings and emotions, the quote above makes perfect sense. Since language is essential for healthy communication, this is a fear that your child must tackle head-on.

Having the confidence to speak your mind and stand up for yourself is crucial in life. In fact, being able to have a **Confidence of Voice** is very important. Believe it or not, confidence is physically powerful and mentally stressful. That's why most adults suppress their feelings and hold back their words. And, as you can probably guess, stress can have negative effects on your health.

How many times have you had an imaginary conversation or argument with your boss, friend, or spouse? Did you say something hurtful or act out? Or, did you remain mum because you didn't have the confidence to speak your truth?

Well, it's important that you instill confidence in your child, so she feels safe enough to speak up and use her words. But, just like with adults, this takes practice and training.

Listed below are some tactics that can help build confidence in your child, so she can communicate more effectively:

First, consider a good martial arts program. This program will help your child develop a **Confidence of Voice** and a **Confidence of Physical Ability**. Your child will learn techniques, and perform katas in front of people, while making "kiais", pronounced kee-eyes, also called spirit yells that are a powerful use of voice.

She will also learn how to recite Dojo Rules and a Student Creed. In addition, she will learn how to speak more fluently in front of classmates, parents, and teachers.

And, little-by-little, she will build her confidence and skills. And, if the program is run efficiently with good instructors, she will become more comfortable there, which will boost her self-esteem. Another plus is that a martial arts program tends to also focus on other skills like: leadership and mentoring. And, you child learns how to speak clearly and concisely in public, and with friends and classmates. She will also learn how to ask effective questions and build a rapport with people. And, once she strengthens her confidence and skills in these areas, she will feel more confident about using her voice in other areas of her life.

It's important that children know early on that it's okay to use their voices. Especially, when things are awkward or uncomfortable. So, explain to her that it's okay to tell people to back up because they are making her uncomfortable. It's also okay to tell someone, if she is afraid, especially if it involves abuse or neglect. Instruct her to tell you, her teacher, a friend, or her coach or martial arts instructor, if someone is doing something to her that she doesn't like. Create a "safe space" for your child and let her know she can always come to you and you will support her. If your child feels safe it will boost her confidence in using her voice.

Sometimes, children can do something on accident that hurts someone else – physically and/or mentally. It's common for children to be scared to face the person they hurt. This stems from a fear to own up to the harm or pain, they caused someone else. So, explain to her the importance of apologizing for wrong-doing. Then, encourage her to reach out to the person she hurt. Now, your child may become nervous or anxious at the prospect of apologizing, but doing it will help build her confidence.

For your child to gain courage, she will have to face the person that she hurt and validate the other person's feelings.

177

So, help your child understand why she is fearful of apologizing by identifying the origin of it. This fear - the fear of facing one's own feelings, falls into the category of **Misplaced Fear**. *Why?* Well, because your child fears what other people will think of her, if she admits fault. She may be afraid that others will view her negatively and call her a jerk or monster – even if what she did was an accident. *So, how can you get your child to tap into her compassion for others? Well, listed below are questions that can start the conversation with your child:*

- How do you think your friend (use the person's name) feels about what happened?

- How do you think *she* (use the person's name) is going to feel, if you **don't** apologize?

- Do you want her to be sad?

- How do you think *she* (use the person's name) will feel, when you apologize to her?

- Even though you are afraid now, when she accepts your apology and gives you hug or handshake with a smile, how do you think you feel?

- Do you think that once you do this and you gain a new confidence that nervous energy will disappear right away? Do you think you will become a stronger, better person because of it?

- Would you like to feel that relief and gain a new power of confidence?

These questions should get your child in the right mindset to act, so remind her that she will be happier once she apologizes. Teach her that it's okay to use her voice. Using her voice will give her more confidence – even if it's confrontational. Learning to communicate effectively with words can also prevent her from holding things in. Holding in emotions can lead to negative self-talk, which is unhealthy. So, teach her to use her voice, as early as possible. As a result, you will have a healthier child - emotionally, mentally, and physically.

CHAPTER FOURTEEN

How Can I Keep My Child from Being a Blind Follower?

"The only thing that will make you happy is being happy with who you are, and not who people think you are. "

~*Goldie Hawn*

You know, no one wants to see their children be a follower, even when he doesn't agree with what's happening – just because he doesn't want to speak up. Maybe, the child lacks **Social Confidence** and/or **Confidence of Voice**, where he doesn't want to speak up because he is afraid that he will lose friends. It's common to tell children that they need to speak up and communicate to others what they will or will not do. Sometimes, a person has to say, "Okay, but I'm not doing that. I'll just do my own thing."

But, one of the hardest things for most people to do is speak their truth to friends, relatives, and loved ones. Some people can express dislikes that stem from outside of their family like work complaints, but find it impossible to confront the people closest to them. Well, children are the exact same way.

Now, I'm not saying it's the worst thing in the world to be a follower – I mean, you can't have a productive tribe if there are only chiefs and no Indians. So, your child can be a follower, but he should choose the right people to follow. Everyone's not going to be a leader. Some people have natural leadership qualities and instincts, while others either develop them later or never at all. But, there's nothing wrong with following a group, if that group is doing good things.

So, don't tell your child *not* to be a follower, if that is what he is inclined to do. Rather, encourage him to associate with a variety of people AND make good friends. The key is to *not* blindly follow or go along with any old group. That's why I like the term, "go-along-er," because it implies that the person is not making a choice, but just going along for the ride with no say or input in where or how fast it goes.

You want your child to make wise choices in life, especially when it comes to his circle of friends. So, if he/ chooses a group of friends, make sure it is a good group, by having your child say the following statements: "I'm choosing to follow you because I like what you are doing. I'm choosing to follow you because I feel like that what you're doing is healthy or beneficial, and it's going to make me better. I'm choosing to follow you because you're good at what I want to be good at. I'm choosing to follow you because I enjoy being your friend, and you are fair and kind."

Contrary to this perspective: "I'm just going along because I'm afraid to tell my friends that I don't want to go along" or "I'll just do it because I don't want to lose my friends." So, to keep your child away from this mentality, actively try to change his mindset. In other words, teach him how to find friends that are more in line with his interests. When you have a "go-along-er," you run the risk of having a child that does things he wouldn't normally do.

For example, if one of your child's "friends" is mean to another child, and your child is "going-along" with these actions, because he wants to fit and not be a target for the other children, he is just as culpable as the mean child. And, as a result, he will probably regret his actions later, but continue to do the same behaviors. And, after a while, he will probably develop a tolerance for the bad behaviors, and as a result, they will no longer bother him.

If you find out that your child is being mean to another child at school, try to get him to reflect on it by drawing his attention to the other person's feelings. Ask your child, "How would you feel if you were the bullied child? What do you think the other child is thinking or feeling right now? Do you want to be a follower or leader? Would a good leader pick on people or bully others? What do you think a confident leader should do if she witnessed someone being bullied or picked on?"

Most children will know the correct answers to these questions. The problem is, at the time, your child is a part of something, so it's hard for him to go against the grain, especially when it comes to his friends. So, he'll most likely go along with what is happening, not thinking about the consequences. He is not making a choice in that moment. He also isn't thinking about the other person's feelings. Some children are naturally more confident and have a more empathy, than others. Confident children will most likely stand up for others, because it's right. So, build as much empathy and confidence in your child. Encourage him to stand up for what's right, even if it's against a group of friends.

And, ask your child the following questions, "Do you want to get in trouble for doing those things?" And, do you want to break the rules just because everyone else is breaking the rules?" And, when your child says, "So-and-so told me to do it." Respond with "Well, now you'll be in trouble just like so-and-so because you listened to a bad leader."

Make sure your child understands that if she is going to be a follower, the leader should worthy of following. Tell her not to go along with a group, simply because she doesn't want to speak up or be independent. As I mentioned before, start teaching your child early on how to speak up and use her voice. Don't forget to explain to your child that it's okay to do things by herself sometimes. It's okay to be independent, an innovator, and the one, who does something first or alone. Because, if your child is enjoying himself, even if she is alone, then other children will want to join her, because they want to have fun too.

Now, at the same time, you don't want your child to be person, who's like, "I don't ever like playing what everyone else likes to play. The other children should do what I want to do – all of the time." There must be a balance. So, explain to your child that if the other children, at recess like to play kickball, she needs to join them sometimes too. Now, she doesn't have to play all of the time. But, always being the one, who sits out, because the others aren't doing what she wants them to do isn't good. It's okay to be agreeable sometimes. This is different than being a "go-along-er." Being agreeable and reasonable means being fair and flexible.

This will strengthen your child's, so she can express her true feelings with confidence. Therefore, teach her how to balance everything, especially when it involves following and leading. And, if for some reason, she is sitting out of everything and doesn't want to participate in any activities, her behavior may be linked to a specific type of fear or lack of confidence. Maybe, she doesn't think she is good at the activities, and as a result, doesn't want to be made fun of by the other children. Or, it could also be that she is simply doesn't want to do it. Regardless, try to identify the reason why your child doesn't want to participate in certain social activities, so you can help her overcome her fear.

CHAPTER FIFTEEN

The Confidence to Stand Up to Bullies

"A successful person is one, who can lay a firm foundation with the bricks that others throw at him or her."

~David Brinkley

This is a complicated topic. There is a huge anti-bullying movement occurring these days. I tend to look at things from the perspective of society and communities, so I believe that any time you have a group of children, it's going to be social. And, in a group, there's always something that comes out. There could be 10 children or 1,000, and if they're together in a group, someone's going to be timid and quieter, and someone else is going to be dominant, outgoing, and more assertive. Everyone has a starting point. In other words, your child will eventually find his place in the pecking order. It's just going to happen, someone will be the leader, and someone's going to be the "right-hand man" to the leader, or the second in charge. Someone's also going to be third in line with the third person being quieter, timider, and shyer than the other children.

When I was a child, a bully was someone everyone deemed mean. Most of my peers were afraid of "the bully." And, some bullies never got in trouble or caught - they were good at what they did. But, most of the time, this behavior stemmed from psychological abuse or psychological warfare. Old-school bullies used to mess with your mind and make you afraid of them. These bullies were slick. They were sneaky and sly. Then, there were the children, who would get into an argument with another student and say something mean once or twice. I don't consider this type of person a bully.

I think being mean towards others is still bad, though. I just don't feel that that is really bullying. Wrong = yes, bullying = no. Bullying, picking, name-calling, physical contact, and exclusion fall under the same umbrella. Bullying is the extreme and may be harder to stand up to and overcome. It takes more confidence, and more courage to stand up to bullies. So, if your child says to you, "Someone made fun of me today." But, that person never makes fun of your child again, it isn't bullying, in my opinion. Still, a one-time event can zap your child's self-esteem and self-confidence. And, even if it's not really mean, but your child feels that it's mean, it can lower his confidence.

It is important to understand that everyone processes insults differently. Some people have thin skin, so they are easily offended, while others have a higher tolerance and are impervious to just about everything. The behaviors in this chapter are no less important than any others, but some are more severe, leading to longer-lasting effects. *So, what is a bully?* Well, a bully is a **Confidence Vampire**. In other words, this person wakes up in the mornings and doesn't feel good about himself, so he victimizes someone else to help him feel better.

A **Confidence Vampire** doesn't have enough confidence to face the things he is afraid of, so he feeds on the victim's fears to get him through the day. In other words, this person doesn't have the confidence or skills to communicate what they are afraid of. He doesn't have a **Confidence of Voice** to speak the truth. He also doesn't have the **Social Confidence** to be nice to people and communicate with people in a nice way.

Bullies look for people they can pick on, then they steal their confidences, like a vampire. They leave their victims feeling drained of confidence, while they feel victorious - revitalized. Bullies get a confidence rush every time they lower the confidences of others - but that's not real confidence. It's **False Confidence**. It's **Stolen Confidence**, and it only lasts a little while. But, bullies look forward to doing this every day.

Here's what you do with a bully – teach your child how to stand up to her. It used to be that a person fought her bully, but that solution is no longer looked upon as the best way to deal with bullying. Although it does work, it's not the most diplomatic way. So, what I tell my students if they are being bullied by **Confidence Vampires**, it is because they have no confidence. They want easy targets. They don't want to put up a fight, and they don't want to get caught or get a lot of attention – they just want to give someone a hard time. The key to blocking these vampires is to stand up to them.

Tell your child not to cooperate or back down. Ironically, most bullies don't want to build confidence or face their fears. So, if your child gives a bully a hard enough time, she will most likely back off. Bullies don't have the confidence or perseverance to make mistakes or fail AND keep trying. Remember, they want easy targets, so if your child becomes a target for a **Confidence Vampire**, but makes it hard for her to feed off her confidence, the vampire won't get her fix for the day.

So, what happens next? Well, most likely, she will just move on to her next victim. See, the thing about bullies is they don't want to put work into tormenting you. It's not supposed to be hard to pick on a person. They want someone they can pick on, and who isn't going to resist, or stand up or have confidence or a voice. That's why they choose people, who have low self-esteem or self-confidence.

So, tell your child that bullies are lazy. Explain to her that bullies don't have confidence, which is why they try to take other people's confidences. Instruct her to stand up against her bully, and tell her, "No." And, keep telling her, "No," regardless of what the bully says or does, or even she pushes her or knock books out of her hands – still tell her, "No." Tell your child that if this situation occurs, simply pick up her books and tell the teacher, you, a coach, or martial arts instructor. Tell someone! Tell your child to use her voice, and I guarantee that the bully will stop harassing her because it's just too difficult. So, tell your child to be difficult and give her bully a really hard time, so she decided it's just too much work and move on.

However, if the bullying turns physical, and your child is too afraid to tell someone what's happening to her, you will need to pay close attention to any changes in her demeanor, behavior, or personality, I've had parents tell me that their children cried and begged them not to send them to school. As a result, the parents became very upset and emotional. Once, the parents found out what was happening to their children, their children begged them not to tell the principals at their schools, because they were afraid the bullies would get in trouble, and there would be repercussions. So, in a case like this, you've got to embolden your child to stand up for herself. Let her know that it's okay to have a voice.

It's hard to coach children through bullying situations, because I'm not around enough to catch the bullying or help them work through it. So, the way I handle bullying with my students is to teach them to ignore the bully. If they can't do that, then I tell them to speak up and resist the bully. After that, I plant the seed of **Confidence of Voice** in them. Unfortunately, the older your child is the more physical and intense, it probably is for him. Once there is physical contact or violence involved, and speaking up isn't working anymore, you need to teach your child that it's okay to defend himself.

It is important to note that bullying doesn't just affect shy children. No, even confident children are susceptible to bullies. Remember, confidence fluctuates, and can increase or decrease, depending on the situation. Remember, even professional athletes lose confidence from time-to-time. Therefore, anyone's confidence can be tested, and broken down.

That's why your goal should be to make sure your child has a strong **Confidence of Voice**. *The story below highlights the effect bullying can have on a shy or insecure child:*

RIAN S.

A little boy named, Rian, was terrified of school bullies, so I helped him come up with a plan, so he would feel comfortable defending himself against his bullies. Well, one day Rian was attacked by three bullies at a school event. He stood his ground, but had no choice but to protect himself against the much bigger and older boys. At first, he didn't want to hurt them, so he held back. But, a few weeks later, they attacked him again. This time, however, Rian refused to hold back and got the better of the boys. After that night, those bullies left him alone and stopped targeting him.

This is a perfect case for having martial arts experience. With martial arts training, your child can learn how to protect himself through blocks and other methods. And, as a result, the bully's intent may be changed without your child having to fight. Self-defense refers to protecting oneself, which will be covered in the next chapter.

So, what I teach at my school is this - *everyone has the right to protect themselves. Never allow anyone to push, pull, hit, kick, punch, or touch you.* Because the truth is as your child gets older, the bullying can become more aggressive, leading to injury.

For instance, if a bully causes your child to bump his head and get knocked out, or fall into a coma, it's too late. I've had parents tell me that their children said to them, "Mom, I didn't want to do anything, because I didn't want to get in trouble." I know Ian said that many times. But, the thing is your child has the right to protect himself. He doesn't automatically have to injure a bully, but he shouldn't let that person injure him either. If your child isn't confident, he runs the risk of being a victim of a bully, but if he is confident, he has a better chance of standing up to him. The more confidence you can build in your child, the more prepared he/ will be in dealing with these types of situations. This will lower your child's risk of being bullied, BUT unfortunately it can't guarantee that he'll never experience it.

CHAPTER SIXTEEN

How Does Martial Arts Build Confidence?

"Get Knocked Down Seven Times, Get Up
Eight!"

~*Ancient Proverb*

Truthfully, martial arts alone probably will not build confidence in your child. It depends on the class or program and the instructors and their level of training, techniques, and understanding of how children learn best. Traditionally, martial arts have helped build confidence through a variety of methods like: repetition and practice, trial and error, failures and mistakes, and working under the guidance of a teacher until the person's skills improved and he became proficient at it.

Little-by-little this person improved. Sometimes it took weeks and sometimes months, but the person felt and saw results. Then, when he became proficient in a technique or skill, it gave him a new confidence. Ironically, in the past, there was very little positive reinforcement in martial arts schools throughout the US, and I'm pretty sure there was probably even less in other countries.

Eventually these schools started to use positive reinforcement to encourage children. They used positive reinforcement to highlight their students' positive traits and pinpointed mistakes, so the students could fix them, and build confidence from learning something new and making progress.

But, even today, if a martial arts instructor says he's teaching confidence that may not be entirely true. Some children may develop confidence from a certain school or martial arts program, but others may not. But, if it is the core of what the instructor does, and it's the golden thread of what he is trying to accomplish, then he should ensure that his students use techniques that will benefit them.

It just comes down to how the school is structured, and what the instructors are trained to do. Building and maintaining confidence in students should be the main goal of the instructors. Together with parents, teachers and coaches, children can gain confidence in a variety of areas.

Teachers should also be cautious about damaging a child's confidence. In fact, some children are confident until their teachers belittle them, yell at them, or criticize them. And, some children, who weren't confident originally, gain confidence over time. With insecure children, all it takes is for a teacher to say something insensitive or hurtful and their confidence declines. So, teachers should take caution when speaking to students and refrain from yelling at them. Remember, children are moldable, so you have an amazing opportunity to really build a strong confidence in your child. Martial arts training is beneficial because it can teach your child balance. You don't want your child to become overly confident, arrogant, or cocky.

Another way a martial arts program can build confidence is by encouraging children to do something new. Every time a person is successful, she builds a new level of confidence. For example, say your child breaks a board for the first time; well, she will gain a new self-confidence instantly. In fact, as soon as your child breaks the board, a light will light up her face, eyes, and body, and her energy will be evident. That's when she gains the confidence. It will be a visible increase in confidence.

The truth is, a lot of children doubt themselves, and feel like they can't break the board. As a teacher, my job is to convince them that they can. So, I may say, " I'm here to support and teach you how to do this. I wouldn't have you do this, if I didn't think you could do it. Just listen to the instructions. If you try your best and you try your hardest, you will break this board. I believe in you and I know you can do this!"

Now, it's important that the board is the appropriate size for the child. And, the instructor must know his students. Then, all he has to do is provide his students with the tools to be successful. The students must have a realistic chance of being successful, however, it shouldn't too easy for them either. A martial arts instructor should give your child as many little victories, as possible, because they will provide your child with a boost of confidence every time.

BOARD-BREAKING

Martial arts also use physical feats and skills like boarding or ice-breaking. These challenges are pretty much pass/fail. You either break it or you don't. You know right away. A person's confidence improves every time she breaks the board. And, performing for an audience and sparring at tournaments can help build confidence. When you go to break a board for the first time, there's an un-known there. There's a fear that you're not going to do it, or you might hurt yourself. But, when you trust your in-structor, and you do what he tells you to do, for the most part, you can do it.

Whether you believed it or not, you can break that board. So, when you see a child break a board for the first time, and her face lights up with energy, it's the best feeling. It's like a new force that wasn't in her before is suddenly there. And, that child will always remember the feeling, because it made her feel fantastic. It's real, because she did it. She broke the board. You didn't break it for her. You didn't lie to her. You didn't tell her it looked good, when it really didn't. She broke it by herself.

Once a student has broken a board and experiences confidence, it becomes a regular way to boost her confidence. She may gain the courage to try new techniques or multiple boards. There's always a way to use board-breaking to build confidence in children. In fact, everyone can benefit from it, because it teaches you how to apply a technique until you become proficient at it.

Don't Build False Confidence

There is false confidence and real confidence. Which one is instilled in the child is up to the instructors. False confidence is usually the result of the parent or teacher wanting the child to succeed and feel good, so they end up helping the child too much or doing it for her. For instance, say a child wants to break the board with her hands, but can't. If she has trouble breaking the board with a technique, then the instructor should have her use another method. In other words, the instructor should find a way for the child to break the board.

It doesn't matter if the child must use her arm, foot, or jumps on it, the instructor should let her break it; so she knows she can do it. This builds true confidence. But, if the instructor snaps it with his own hands, and the child believes she broke it by herself – that's **False Confidence**. This type of confidence isn't helpful, because it's not real. The problem is when the child tries to break the board the next time; she may not be able to do it, lowering her self-esteem and confidence. She was tricked by the instructor. So, I am not very big on giving others **False Confidence**, especially with children. So, if a child is doing something wrong, it's the instructor's responsibility to tactfully tell her the truth.

The instructor should also use the PCP (Praise-Correct-Praise) technique with the child. It will make it easier for her to accept the criticism. The instructor should highlight something positive the child did, and offer corrections and suggestions to help her build **Physical Confidence**.

LEARNING NEW SKILLS

This includes breaking-boards or trying new things that your child hasn't done before. As I mentioned in previous paragraphs, at martial arts schools, your child is required to perform katas in front of people. If it's at the school, he does this in front of instructors and the class. If it's at a tournament, he does it in front of an audience.

It can be nerve-wracking to do these things in front of others, but with practice, you child can build confidence. He will become more comfortable with each outing. And, eventually, his fear will subside. Facing fears can help your child build confidence.

Another aspect of the tournaments is kumite or fighting matches. Your child is also required to do this in front of people. During these matches an opponent hits him. Most children are afraid to spar, because, like board-breaking, they've never done it before. However, in this case, they don't want to get hurt, because someone's trying to hit or kick them. Most of the time, no one gets hurt, because of safety gear and supervision, however, it's still scary for most children.

Every time someone performs a task successfully, without experiencing what he feared, he gains a little more confidence. Getting over the fear of being hurt, during a sparring match occurs once he realizes that he will not get hurt. Sometimes, however, children get the wind knocked out of them. That's when they get jittery, but eventually they get back in there, for the most part, if they have good instructors that encourage them to continue. When your child becomes good at sparring and fighting, he gains another level of confidence.

Learning new techniques, perfecting old ones, breaking-boards or doing things your child has never done before are measurable and visible. A student can feel them, the teacher and peers can see them, and you can measure your child's progress by them. The good thing is your child can tell if he is improving and if the techniques is working. Performing in front of people, and embracing **Physical Fears** helps increase confidence.

TEACHERS

Lastly, you have the instructors, who can give positive reinforcements and remind your child of her achievements. This always helps. It's reinforcement, but, again, it's important that teachers make sure that they are honest with their students. Teachers shouldn't tell them they're doing a good job, when they're not. They also shouldn't let their students think they are doing great all the time. If it's honest, true feedback, and they did something well, teachers should tell them that, but also tell them why. Don't just say, "Hey, that was awesome, Man! Good job, Billy!"

Teachers can do that with young children, but as they get a little older, they need explanations. In this case, the teacher should say, "That was great" and then ask them, "Do you know why it was great?" They probably won't know, but some may. Then, she should tell them. They need it pointed out to them, so they remember. When children hear the teacher say they did an awesome job, they're going to be so happy that they did well that it's going to automatically boost their confidences. It is a type of conditioning. They'll have a revelation or make the connection and say to themselves, "Oh, if I do this, it is going to be good, and then maybe, I can get the reinforcement or approval from my teacher or parents." The children shouldn't be praised all the time by their teachers, but when they do it, they should explain to them why they are receiving the praise.

Remember, not all schools and teachers are equal, so make sure you do your homework, and check out the report, "*How Do I Pick the Right Martial Arts School for Me and My Child for Confidence?*"

CHAPTER SEVENTEEN

Do All Martial Arts Build Confidence?

"Confidence is the most important single factor in this game, and no matter how great
your natural talent, there is only one way to
obtain and sustain it – through work."

~Jack Nicklaus

*Can all martial arts instructors
build confidence in students?* The answer is "No." I'm isolating martial arts
separately from coaches and sports, because many people bring their children
to martial arts, so that they can build
confidence, so I'm making a separate
chapter on this. The reason all martial
arts instructors don't build confidence in
students is because some instructors
teach an old-school way. They tend to
yell at students and exhibit aggression
towards them. It's negative reinforce-

ment and criticism, and it's not productive for learning.

There is a reason people taught that way long ago. It was effective at the time, but now, instructors, like me, don't have to do that. When you teach someone like that, it's almost impossible for him to make corrections. In the past, instructors were short on words, when giving corrections. They used bamboo sticks to hit people, when they made mistakes. Instead of telling the student repeatedly, they would just hit him on the spot/body part, where he made the mistake. The pain would prompt the student to fix his mistakes quicker. It wasn't meant to be cruel, but the instructors had limited time, and there was an urgency to ensure that the students could protect or defend themselves on the battlefield.

The instructors didn't have time to nurture students and spoon-feed them lessons. That type of teaching style carried over into modern times. Although, it was effective at getting the result at the time, it no longer fits. An instructor can't be mean to students and tell them that their kicks don't look good or they will be White Belts forever. Sadly, though there are still a lot of schools that use outdated practices.

They're not with the times, as far as understanding the psychology of children and teaching the most effective way. When you only point out mistakes and not the positives, it can affect a person's confidence, regardless of whether they are an adult or child. Therefore, an instructor should make sure that he is pointing out both things, positive and negative. If he only highlights the bad, his students will become discouraged. Of course, instructors usually don't say, "I'm going to teach you this way, because we don't have time." Or, "I'm going to teach you this way to speed up the process." They just leave you hanging with a bunch of negative feedback, and that's hard for a lot of people to overcome.

I've experience times, when my instructor told me my mistakes in a nice way, but only pointed out the mistakes. I remember saying to him, "Man, am I doing anything right?" Then, I caught myself! I wanted to hear positive feedback, because I was letting the critical feedback negatively affect me. It wasn't negative feedback, it was the feedback that I needed to correct my mistakes. The instructor was just pointing out the pieces that were flawed, so I could fix them.

Part of me wanted to hear him say something positive or be excited about something I did well. I knew it would make me feel better, but it would not make my technique better. I understand the psychology of it, but at times, it still affects me when I'm critiqued. So, if an adult can be affected in this way, imagine a child with confidence that is still malleable, experiencing that same situation.

As an instructor, you think it's nothing, but it is. We are responsible for the emotional states and confidence levels of our students. Our job is to encourage and inspire them to want to do better. Sometimes, they need a nudge. You don't force children to do things they don't want to do, but sometimes you've got to nudge them in the right direction.

For instance, if you want your child to play basketball or work on drills say, "Come on, let's work on drills. Or, let's go practice." Then, you can go outside and start. After a while your child will start emulating you. That's how children learn best. There are many children in martial arts that lack confidence. These students don't have the tough layer needed to take the negative feedback or yelling, so they end up with even lower self-confidence. Truthfully, these children's confidence may be in jeopardy in this type of environments. It is sad that the children, who need martial arts the most are weeded out by certain schools and martial arts instructors.

People go to martial arts schools, specifically for discipline and confidence. You can't criticize and ridicule a child's technique, because she'll lose confidence. Therefore, it's important that you do your homework and research, so you can find martial arts schools with good instructors. Ask the instructors how they teach children, what kind of material and curriculum they cover, disciplinary methods, and how they interact with families. All these things are important. Then, you'll get a quality martial arts program. You don't want to just go to one, where everyone's nice and they're great with the children, but they're not teaching them anything effective or useful. You've got to find one that has all of these things.

As a parent, you need to do your homework, and instructors should learn as much as they can from the available material on effective teaching. I recommend the podcast from Melody Shuman of Skillz. Also, download the report on how to find the best martial arts school for your family. This report outlines what is considered well-rounded schools. Remember, a quality martial arts school offers quality training, builds confidence in your child, even the shy ones, and provides a healthy social environment for her. *Download it here.*

CHAPTER EIGHTEEN

Sports and Coaches

"When you have confidence, you can have a lot of fun. And when you have fun, you can do amazing things."

~*Joe Namath*

Sports can have positive or negative effects on confidence. There is no way to determine, if sports alone can build confidence in an individual. It is quite possible that the experience diminishes confidence or discourages children. A lot of it has to do with the coaches, and the methods they use, and of course, the child's current confidence level. Another factor to consider is social interactions with the other children on the team.

The ideal situation would be to use sports to build confidence in all the participants. Building confidence should be a mandatory part of coaching and teaching children. To build confidence, it should be made the main goal. The right type of coach is needed to implement in an effective plan to build the players' confidences.

These methods must be supportive to the players, flexible, and universal to everyone's confidence levels. It is important that the teachers not inadvertently crush students or break them down early in the process of teaching, or risk losing an opportunity to make a great impact on them. There is a bell curve when it comes to people. This is true for different types of confidence, and confidence, overall. You may know super sensitive individuals, who are not able to take criticism from coaches very well. *Super Confidence Academy* provides exercises, tactics, and strategies that can help build your child's confidence.

Download them at: www.superconfidenceAcademy.com.

Remember, it is your job is to ensure that your child builds confidence. **Social Confidence** is one of the main types of confidence that can be influenced and affected by sports, because it requires children to interact with teammates and opponents. Now, that doesn't mean your child will get along with everyone, but he will learn how to deal with different types of personalities. Sports provides a social environment, where children can sharpen their communication and social skills. They can also make new friends and get to know people.

Therefore, coaches should encourage players to get to know each other, and treat each other with respect. This can be done using friendly competition and team-building exercises to maximize the connection between players. If your child is in a member-based activity like martial arts, gymnastics, or dance, they must interact with teammates and opponents. Some of the programs offer extra events like: "movie night," or special training seminars, which provide opportunities for teammates to bond.

These events are designed to help teammates develop new friendships and strengthen social bonds between the students and members. The children have an opportunity to strengthen their **Social Confidences** during the events. At my martial arts school, we encourage children to introduce themselves to new students. This is done to prevent the new students from feeling out of place and uncomfortable. It makes a difference to new students. In fact, it helps them become more confident in the new environment.

If a child really wants to make a competitive sports team, but is put through paces by the other players, until she proves herself that is understandable. And, although, some can take the heat because they have **Confidence of Will** and **Confidence in Physical Ability**, others just don't have confidence to be successful. Regardless, sports can also build the confidence to overcoming fear and trying again, especially when your child is learning a new skill. When she performs things that are new to her, she develops confidence every time that she performs the skill successfully. In addition, every time this happens, her brain recognizes that the skill was performed correctly, and this reward increases her **Confidence in Physical Ability**.

Even more powerful is when someone else points out that the skill has improved. Recognition of a skill boosts confidence tremendously for children. Therefore, sports play a big part in helping children build confidence. The hard part is when a child didn't do well, or she compares herself to other children. Children, who lack **Confidence of Self-Image** and **Confidence of Will** may be just as good as the other children, but their minds tell them they are inferior.

Sports can also take away confidence, if the child cannot perform well. Just encourage him to keep going and not give up. Playing sports is a good way to strengthen his character. Therefore, sports train children for real life. For example, a person might swing at 30 pitches and get 29 strikes, before he or she hits one ball. With perseverance and the **Confidence to Overcome and Try Again,** and practice, her hitting ability will go up.

It is up to you and your "village" to keep children motivated and trying. You shouldn't let your child quit, when something becomes challenging. Don't allow your child to quit, because he's not doing so well, or it's no longer fun, because it only does a disservice to his confidence. If you encourage your child to keep trying and show him how to overcome mistakes, it will improve his self-esteem. Just pay attention to the look on his face when he starts improving and attaining little victories like: making shots, hitting the ball, etc. This experience is priceless for everyone involved.

COACHES

Coaches play a big role in our children's confidence. Therefore, it's time coaches start thinking about the lasting effects they have on children. Coaches should improve their effectiveness by learning, as much as possible about their crafts. They should read coaching books written by championship coaches and professional coaches. And, add books on mindset, child development, success, child phycology books, and learning styles to their collections.

Moreover, they should attend seminars, listen to podcasts, and/or watch documentaries on successful coaches.

They need to teach children better. This involves structuring practices and drills. This knowledge is essential, if youth sports or academic programs are going to evolve and become even more successful. Acquiring this knowledge and information will assist coaches in putting together drills that will be more fun. A lot of the coaches try to teach children at levels that are outside of their stages of development. They teach younger kids, as if they process like their older counterparts. Many coaches verbally give instructions to four and five-year-olds and think that they will be able to produce the desired outcomes by listening, as if they were experienced players.

They're teaching at a level above what is acceptable for young beginners. There are a few problems with that. First, it's brings down the confidence of children, who can't process the verbal instructions. On numerous occasions, I have witnessed coaches talking for 10-13 minutes, to 5-year-olds about skills that were way above their heads.

Out of 30 kids, maybe three understood what was being asked of them. The ones, who happened to catch on, were the coach's children, and even they had trouble.

The second issue is the time that is spent using words. Twelve-minutes is way too long to talk to 5-year-olds about play, if you want them to pay attention. In this case, half of the time was spent on an angry coach scolding young children about not listening or paying attention. Unfortunately, they couldn't because it was outside of their abilities, but the coach was not aware of this.

Group or class size is another thing to keep in mind. The student-to-coach ratio must make sense. The structure of the drills must be optimized to get the most out of the number of coaches compared to the number of children. If you have a large group, poor structure, and organization with limited coaches, it will inevitably lead to frustration on both sides. If the students don't understand the instructions, because of the way it's being communicated, they will become frustrated, and the coaches will get frustrated, leading to discouraged children with low confidences. So, to coach children, one must understand the mind of a child.

If you talk over 10-minutes to a group of five-year-olds about anything, baseball, rugby, wrestling, etc., they are not going to listen to you. They're going to zone out and fade away within the first two minutes or maybe sooner. These children will probably start daydreaming about something else and forget everything you said. If you ask them what you said, they're going to respond with "I don't know."

Of course, they don't get it, and it's not their faults, because their brains can't process that much info at one time. Maybe, one or two can, but they are the exceptions. So, if a coach tells children that she wants them to practice a skill, most will be bored, but say, "Okay." They need to be inspired to practice, which means it needs to be fun.

Coaches need to pay attention to things like tone of voice and the words they use to communicate to players. Most importantly, they need to be mindful of their patience with them. There may come a time, when they need to raise their voice to get the players' attention and that is okay, if it is done in a controlled manner and not in anger. But, it's still important that coaches learn to accept minor mistakes and learn how to critique players, especially the younger ones. When dealing with children, coaches should avoid showing them their frustration, because it will crush them.

And, they should keep in mind that children make mistakes, so correcting them in front of others only makes them self-conscious, which is counterproductive. The goal is to communicate a solution to them that will help them understand how to fix their mistakes. That's why sometimes, it is best to do this at a different time, maybe the next practice, depending on the child. Coaches also need to reinforce the players' accomplishments. This will strengthen their **Confidence of Physical Ability, Confidence of Will,** and **Confidence of Self-Image.**

As the players mature, coaches can be more direct. They can let them know that they didn't execute, but also explain how they can avoid mistakes, as individuals and as a team. They can teach the players about failures and losses with courage. Because, it is in them that you will find the seeds of growth and success.

It is easy for coaches to get excited about raw talent or athletic confidence, but they need to be cautious about crushing the confidence of the players, who are not naturally athletic and of weeding out the shy ones. They need to give the shy, less confident children a chance to benefit from the process of learning something new and being part of a team. Just because someone is shy doesn't mean he is not athletic. Maybe, he just doesn't have the **Social Confidence** to shine in a group. Maybe, they are fast runners, maybe they can catch, or maybe they have great hand-eye coordination, but just need practice to feel comfortable. They may be seeds waiting to become awesome athletes, but coaches never give them a chance. And, if a coach knocks down their confidences, they miss out on the next Michael Jordan.

CHAPTER NINETEEN

You Were Born with Confidence and
Perseverance of a True Champion!

"Our deepest fear is not that we are inade-
quate. Our deepest fear is that we are powerful beyond measure. It is our light, not our
darkness that most frightens us. We ask ourselves, who am I to be brilliant, gorgeous, talented, and fabulous? Actually, who are you
not to be? You are a child of God. You're playing small does not serve the world. There is
nothing enlightened about shrinking so that
other people won't feel insecure around you.
We are all meant to shine, as children do.
And, as we let our own light shine, we uncon-
sciously give other people permission to do
the same. As we are liberated from our own
fear, our presence automatically liberates others."

~*Marianne Williamson*

It is time to tap into to the confidence and greatness of your child. If your child has made it to the finish line called "life," you are doing something right. I am only referring to the attributes distributed to you by the forces of creation, not your placement in this world, as it pertains to status, family, or fortune. You are a champion; therefore, your child is to. *All people have some confidence, but what would you think if I told that we were all born with the same level of confidence?* Human beings come into this world, as very confident individuals with a high level of perseverance and determination. As a matter of fact, we all come into this world with drive and determination.

So, let's return to the driving force of human nature. Let's look at what happens before we are born. During conception, your parents combined two life-producing elements to create you and bring you into the world. Your mother provided the egg and your father, the sperm. Recent research suggests that the release of an egg, depends on the environment, and the mother's comfort-level and stress level. The father releases 40 million to 1.2 billion sperm. Forget one in a million, you were one in billion or maybe more! You were designed to be a champion.

For you to be who you are, it took generations of the right people getting together and procreating, and then your parents meeting and doing the same. Then, you had to win that race. You don't know how close the race was, and it doesn't matter. You could have been someone else. It could have been a different sperm that made it to the egg, but it wasn't. You beat out millions and billions of competitors, and ultimately reached your goal - life.

Think about this, you made it through a hostile environment, before you were finally born. *Who taught you how to walk? Who taught you how to stand? Some will say moms, and some will say dads, but did your parents teach you and support your efforts along the way?* Your parents taught you certain things, but no one can teach a baby how to walk. A baby cannot follow instructions, due to a very limited vocabulary. *So, how did you learn how to walk?* You taught yourself! You taught yourself how to walk. The same goes for crawling and standing. This process included many tries, mistakes, and failures - including falling down.

A child will have many failed attempts during this process, and I believe that's why your actual memory of that time is blocked. You don't remember that period, because you experienced too much failure, too many mistakes, non-stop falling, every day, all day. That would be difficult for anyone to be able to deal with. Think about the number of times a baby falls in their pursuit of walking and standing. Constantly, falling and getting bumped and bruised. As toddlers transition, they go through this for months, maybe a year, then they start walking.

At this stage, you are laser-focused on doing what you desire, which is to stand and then walk. You are not trying to do it, but you are in the process of doing it. You have the support of your parents, because they want you to succeed at walking. They smile at you and encourage you. And, when they support you, it feels good. You have an additional motivation to keep going. There is the reward of recognition.

Eventually, children walk. They do this through their own powers of observation, copying, and an **Innate Confidence of Will**. A few years back a friend of mine said something very interesting. She said, "More is caught, then taught." And, I find this to be very true! So, if you want your child to do something, do it first and allow him to copy you. If you appear to be having fun, your child will want to do it too.

You weren't taught how to walk or stand by anyone, you taught yourself and kept going. You walked until you could do it, and then you ran. You never gave up, even though you fell a few times, and were afraid to fall again. You never saw a fall, as a fail, because every fall was a lesson that got you one step closer to your goal of walking. In every fall, in every failure, and in every mistake, there was a lesson that helped you progress further.

Every time you fell, you tried again and again and again. And, every time your brain made new neurological connections that helped you understand balance, coordination, and movement. It took hundreds, maybe thousands of falls to get you to your goal. The confidence achieved at every victory was visible on your toddler face! And, that additional confidence fueled your desire to continue and learn more.

We all have the potential to tap into that well of perseverance, drive, and determination. We just must remember the things, we have accomplished, and how difficult it would be to learn those things now, as compared to when we were younger. We have learned so many things, as we have grown. This is your potential. It's what you're capable of. You can do anything.

You can teach yourself anything. But, at some point, it is hidden from you. You lose it, usually between the ages of 3-6, right around the time you can effectively communicate.

You are given an opportunity to use this amazing power for a short time, and then you find it again. But, very few people ever get back to that same level of perseverance. It's like God saying, "If you can find you can have it, after all, it is yours to possess."

Confidence is something we all have, we were all born with the same level of it. Once we can finally get that into our minds, there will be nothing we can't have or achieve. Nothing can get in the way of our success, if we regain this innate power. The only one that can get us that way is us! The ability to find and use this gift we all have, plays a large part of how confident and successful we become. Remember the saying, "If you think you can, or if you think you can't, you're right." Whatever you believe in and whatever you think you can do, you can do.

If you think you can, you're right, because if you start trying, you're already doing it. If you're trying to learn a skill, you're doing the skill, you're just not doing it well. But, you're already doing it. If you want to start trying, then you can. If you think you can't, and you don't try, then you can't. You're right either way. The difference between the two is your mindset, a confident mindset.

It's about having an "I can" attitude, rather than an "I can't" attitude. If you have an "I can" attitude, it's going to take you farther in life. We were all born with an "I can" attitude. Therefore, we can watch the world around us and teach ourselves how to walk, talk, and stand.   If we can find our innate child-like confidence, we can do great things. And, if we can teach our children to hold onto this power, we can produce some incredibly confident human beings.

Reference: Olsen, E. R. (2013). Sperm count: Why are 250 million sperm cells released during sex? *Life's Little Mysteries*.

About the Author

Arthur Hearns is a life coach, martial arts and fitness entrepreneur, public speaker and author. Starting as a professional personal trainer in 1991, he began helping people transform their bodies and minds by helping them overcome their fears and found that this gave them a new level of confidence.

In 2005 he opened Hands of Life Martial Arts Academy. This allowed him to fulfill his dream of being a teacher who could impact people lives in a positive way. Since then he has helped thousands improve their focus, respect, self-control, improve their health and of course, confidence. Through Hands of Life he has been able to give 10's of thousands of dollars to charities, local schools and local community causes.

A native of New Jersey, Hearns is the father of two fantastic boys who he enjoys drawing and being creative, creating new knock-knock jokes, playing sports, going to the movies and lightsaber dueling with.

Still an active student in the martial arts, Hearns trains with his own teacher twice per week. An avid skier, Hearns confidently took up skiing at the age of 35 and is now an expert level skier. He is also a certified I.A.N.T.D Scuba Diver.

To book Arthur Hearns at your next event, speaking engagement, seminar, podcast or live video contact him at arthur@ArthurHearns.com or support@superconfidenceacademy.com. Call or text 732-735-4876.

The author with his two sons. Building and practicing confidence, while having fun!

Made in the USA
Middletown, DE
09 May 2018